SCARLET embodies the disembodied, earthy and ethereal experience of pandemic shock. Searing seer unfurls a lyric documentary here. Each page sings and singes with koans of unfolding insight: "When you've/ no more and you've/ suddenly stopped/ on a/ fitted arrow."

The words dwell within the frame of an apocalyptic pandemic imagined by a past Californian author, eerily pointing to deadly patterns revivified ad infinitum. Glitches, blots, words overlapping and erased, bits of words peeking out, (peaking with sound) exemplify the human experience of attempting to process and surmise a new physical (and digital) reality. "I remember it/ spat loudly/ the word/ a strange disease that had/ broken out."

In this ruminative work, words float through the Bardo state we are collectively inhabiting. Though the matter is dark, the stark words arise out of the page's earthy colors, allowing the reader grace and space to absorb pain.

At the most primal level, *Scarlet* embodies our fight for survival:

"we ground on/ eyes down/ It was more about getting food"

"left little to take away"

Our attempts to cope—superstitious and bewildered:

"Spit when you cross/ to keep off bad luck"

"don't know how/ to/ Let go"

Scarlet employs technocracy as healing agency while also aware of its limitations. What is lost poetically, metaphysically?

"that light on you/ interrupted"

A dirge for our lost intimacy:

> "It is/ years since I have/ seen You"

Eco-poetics are also present, an abiding awareness of Earth's pangs:

> "the/ heat of/ the spreading like wildfire"

> "the flood/ sweeping handiwork/ away"

> "like the last days/ of/ gasoline"

Scarlet, a color, both bloody and signifying a dictator:

> "red year"

> "Mingled with the/ roar/ a continuous, deep-/ throated barking/ a jagged/ lie/ a/ fire, tended savage"

> "a mass of /population, mad from fear and/ fires raging."

> "censoring news"

> "Strange and terrible sights/ slipped by"

In many ways the poem feels like an expression of the Hell-realms experienced, replete with hungry ghosts and images of bodies, hot from a funeral pyre:

> "fell to / as/ it must/ Scarlet/ and/ alive"

> "skeletons exposed./ everywhere run-/ inng from contagion"

> "bodies everywhere,/ not yet /smoke"

> "bodies/ increased/ countless and/ packed together"

The "We" takes centerstage in *Scarlet*, as we share the common experience of suffering. The "I" is seen in brief moments, as a pathway to comprehend what

We lost: "he/ died./ there were no lights,/ no more being/ I heard/ the glare of sky." This is a hauntingly compassionate work, a balm for our world sorrow, highly empathizing with the beings undone, the millions of lives unsung in this unsettling time.

—Heather Woods, author of *Bundling*

When I was a child, I learned the word "opaque" from a package of ballet tights. But after my mother explained that opaque meant unable to see through, I couldn't understand why the opaque ballet tights still showed through— they didn't block all sight or light, as the word advertised, and it was only later I learned that no, they were only opaque relative to the more common "sheers" still worn daily by women in the 1970s of my youth. That this sort of relative opacity posited its own gendered universe was lost on me at the time—as Francesco Levato's *Scarlet* says, "I was overwhelmed with sight." The best art is similarly obfuscated, as Bernadette Mayer had it, "The best obfuscation bewilders old meanings while reflecting or imitating or creating a structure of a beauty that we know." (*The Obfuscated Poem*). In Levato's multivalent cross-out of Jack London's 1912 novel using the 1917 Victor Shklovsky technique to "defamiliarize" our 2020s un-reality, Levato and *Scarlet* collaborate to morph daily objects into abstracted smears, peeling sentences apart to reveal their veined interiors. Levato shakes the poetry from the prose, asking us to view the quotidian as altered as we are. The titles themselves are still lives of objects in uncanny juxtaposition, seen anew and uncommon and fitting—Crown Royal bag and bronzed baby shoe—while the poems that bleed through the pages ask about the culpability of language in our pandemic-laced trauma, the onus of communication erased, information unshared. With an eye and ear inside the machine that is the book, Levato reveals "the jagged lie" under the "continuous deep-throated barking" that contained both "more than we knew" and "if anything, nothing." Years on and years to come, Levato beautifully and structurally understands that we will forever wear the pandemic not as a metaphor but as a bewilderingly opaque sheer, another skin.

—Sandra Doller, author of *Leave Your Body Behind*

"A connection... lifted... into view." Levato's *Scarlet* magnificently captures the withered yet still holding social and textual connections between us during the first years of the Covid 19 pandemic. Using language processing techniques like erasures and, more importantly, semi-erasures, Levato discovers networks between primary, subsidiary, and subterranean vocabularies and uses his discoveries to inscribe an apocalyptic yet all too necessary togetherness we grasped at during the terrible first months and years of the 2020s.

—Mark Nowak, author of *Social Poetics*

The table of contents could be read as an anxious list poem of pandemic preoccupations and activity. The combination of glitched photos of everyday life during lockdown and erasures of the text of a dystopian novel written in the early twentieth century is an effective and artful way to represent the pandemic years of our time. The murkiness of the muted and dark colours of the images and the abstractions of the glitched artefacts gave me the feeling of swimming underwater, slowly making my way through unknown depths. The erasure's disruption of existing narrative evokes the disjointed and troubling feelings of the Covid-19 pandemic, especially in the first lockdowns. Reading *Scarlet*, I had a sense of truth being stranger than fiction. What London predicted in his 1912 novel has come to pass. Levato has skillfully and sensitively carved current fact and feeling out of another writer's prescient imagination. *Scarlet* gives me feelings of connection, recognition, and relief in a disturbing and anxious millennium. In a world where nothing makes sense, the book feels like an attempt at sense making. It pieces together what is fragmented, indecipherable, unknown, and frightening. In using the techniques of glitch and erasure, Levato is also playing. I like to imagine that it was fun and satisfying to make these poems.

—Amanda Earl, Editor of *Judith, Women Making Visual Poetry*

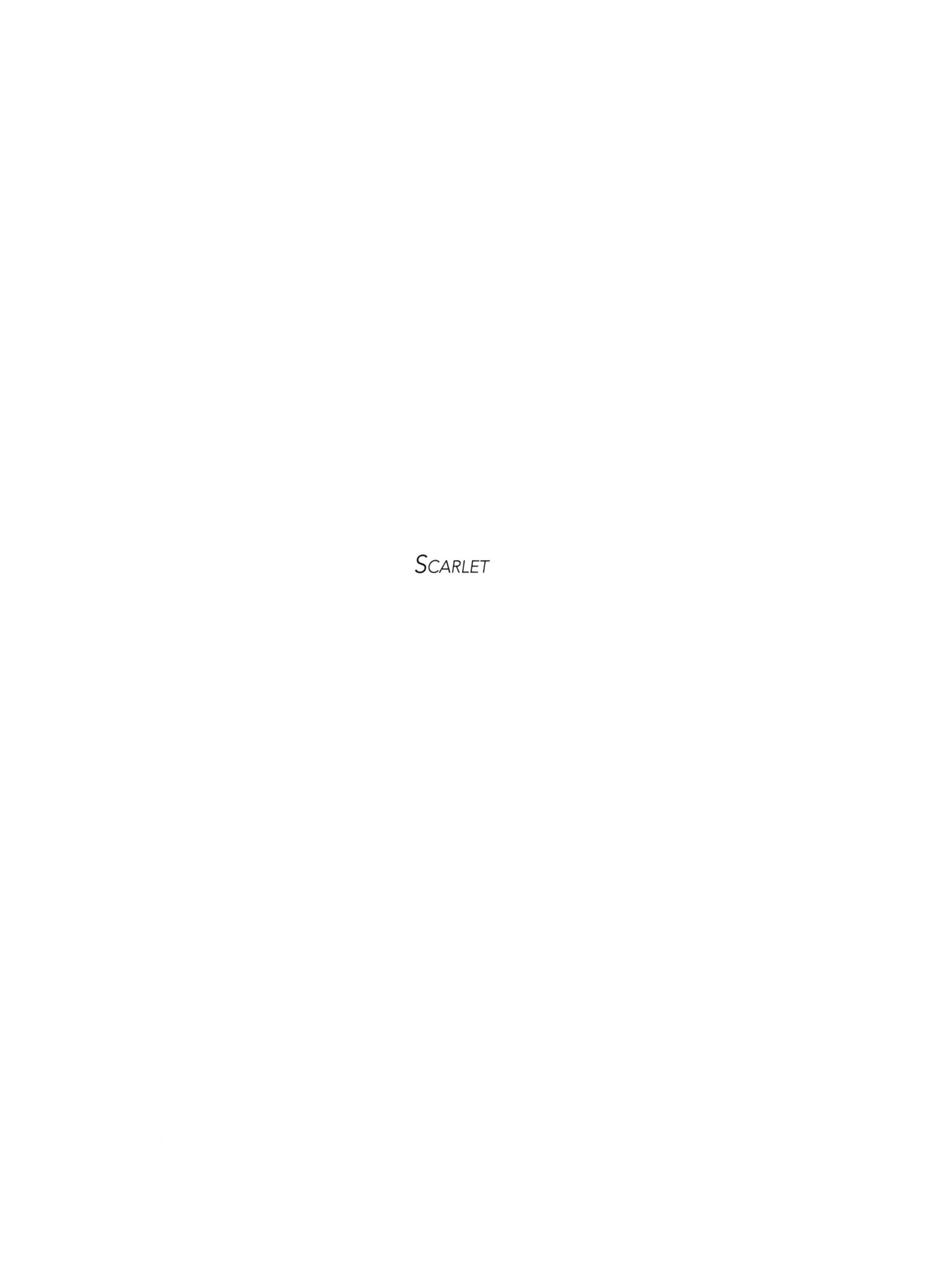

SCARLET

SCARLET

Francesco Levato

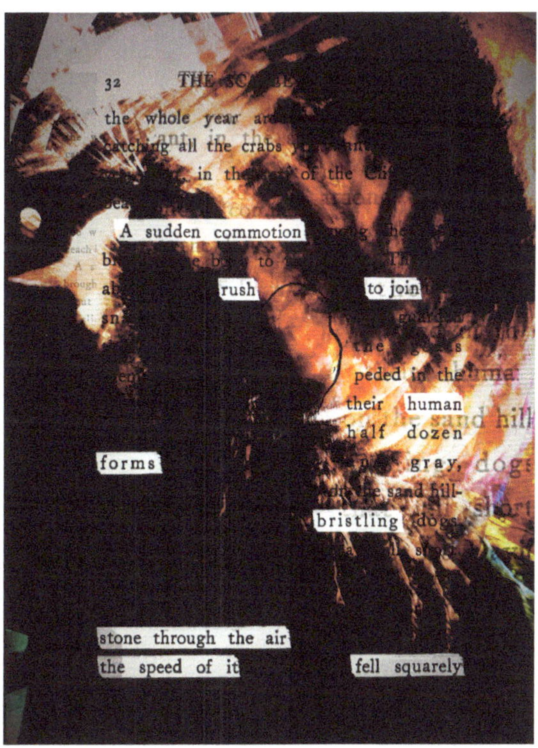

SPUYTEN DUYVIL
NEW YORK CITY

Acknowledgements:

With thanks to the editors of DISGUST: Unhealthy Practices, East Window Gallery, Experiment-O, FERAL, FIVES: A Companion to Denver Quarterly, Harpy Hybrid Review, Heavy Feather Review, IceFloe Press: Pandemic Dispatches, Imposter, Matter, Posit, Scapegoat Review, Star 82 Review, The Conjuncture, The Indianapolis Review, The New Verse News, Train, and Unlost Journal, where some of these poems first appeared.

Library of Congress Control Number: 2023941767

SCARLET began as a digital visual/poetic meditation on the psychological and physical toll of social isolation during the COVID-19 lockdown. The project then evolved to document the social, political, and personal disruption of the pandemic as we moved through its various mutations and surges.

The digital/visual poems are created through erasure of the novel *The Scarlet Plague*, by Jack London, collaged with glitched imagery from everyday life during the pandemic. The titles of poems in the series are derived from objects contained in each glitched still life.

Glitching is a technique that introduces errors into the code of a digital file or stream that distorts its presentation. The error-induced fracturing of images in *SCARLET* is intended to defamiliarize everyday objects and surroundings to reflect the psyche under the constant stress of the pandemic.

The Scarlet Plague is a post-apocalyptic novel, published in 1912, set in California during the year 2073, after the world's population is decimated by an uncontrollable pandemic.

Closet with Raincoat & Plastic Crate   1

Pitcher, Plate, French Toast   2

Cutting Board & Chamomile   3

Skin, Syringe, Latex Gloves   4

Medicinal Tea, 4 a.m.   5

Chiromancy & Kali   6

Bookshelf, with Witch Hazel & Rope Basket   7

Package Delivery, through Screen Door   8

Skeleton, Seated, with Coriander   9

Workspace with Coffee Mug   10

Self-Portrait with Bauhaus   11

Unpacking   12

Mask, Red   13

Three of Swords   14

Trash Can with Cat Vomit & Coffee Grounds   15

Go Bag, Jump Starter, Bottled Water   16

Nightstand with Gargoyle, Kava, and CBD Oil   17

Refrigerator with Cup, Near Empty   18

Cacti through Closed Window   19

Tattoo with Tentacles   20

Self-Portrait with Pixies   21

Self-Portrait, 4 a.m.   22

Masks, Gloves, Goggles   23

Front Room with Dried Eucalyptus & Vinyl   24

Countertop with Dirty Dishes   25

Barcode, Notepad, Hospital Bracelet   26

Margot   27

Self Portrait, with Planets   28

Bare Floor, with Coat Hanger   29

Self Portrait, in Fragments   30

Stockpile with Non-Perishable Food   31

Moving Box, Incomplete   32

Green Glass Bottle, Christmas Ornaments   33

Living Room, with Stage Props   34

Bookshelf with Dante & Wax Seal   35

Cabinet with Hand Sanitizer & Alcohol Wipes   36

Discarded Mask, Parking Lot C   37

Roadside, Hiking Shoe, Discarded Mask   38

Hell-On   39

Still Life with Crown Royal Bag & Bronzed Baby Shoe   40

Test Card, Swab, Single Purple Line   41

Session 0   42

Stunted Apples, Homegrown   43

Parking Lot, with Discarded Surgical Mask   44

Knife Block with Flask   45

Flag on Pole, Inert   46

Self Portrait, After Campus Return   47

Tattoo, Wrist, Scars   48

Cereal, Skull Cup, Blueberries   49

Rx Bottles, Bedspread   50

Air Filter, Fan, Power Strip   51

Caffè Macchiato, Cloth Napkin   52

NyQuil, Cough Drops, Government-issue COVID Tests   53

Test Card, Extraction Reagent, Nasal Swab   54

Carved Wooden Doll Head   55

Markstein Hall 250   56

Obituary   57

Bela Lugosi's Dead   58

Coffee, with Course in General Linguistics   59

Godzilla vs. Ghidorah, S.H. Monster Arts   60

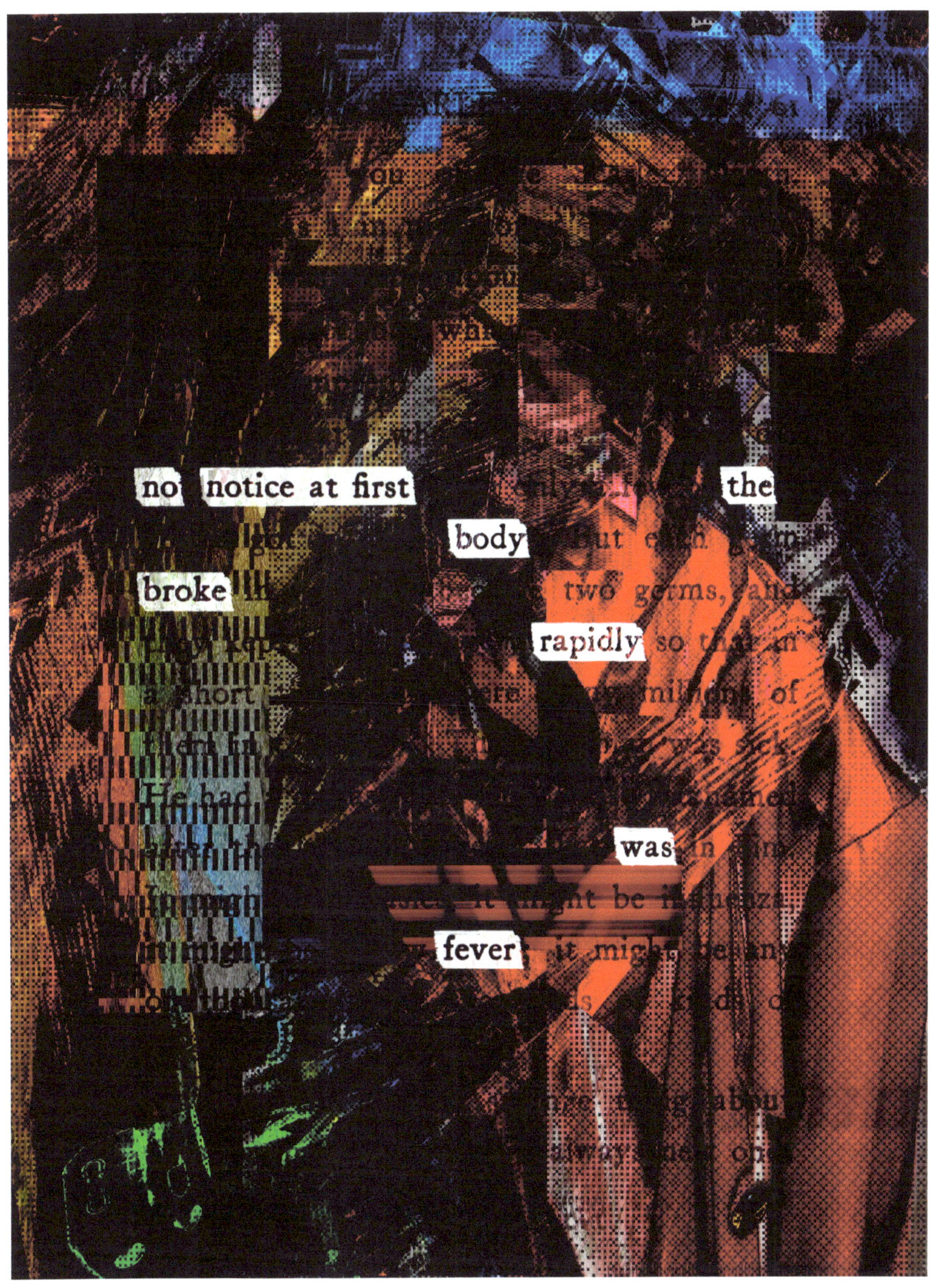

CLOSET WITH RAINCOAT & PLASTIC CRATE

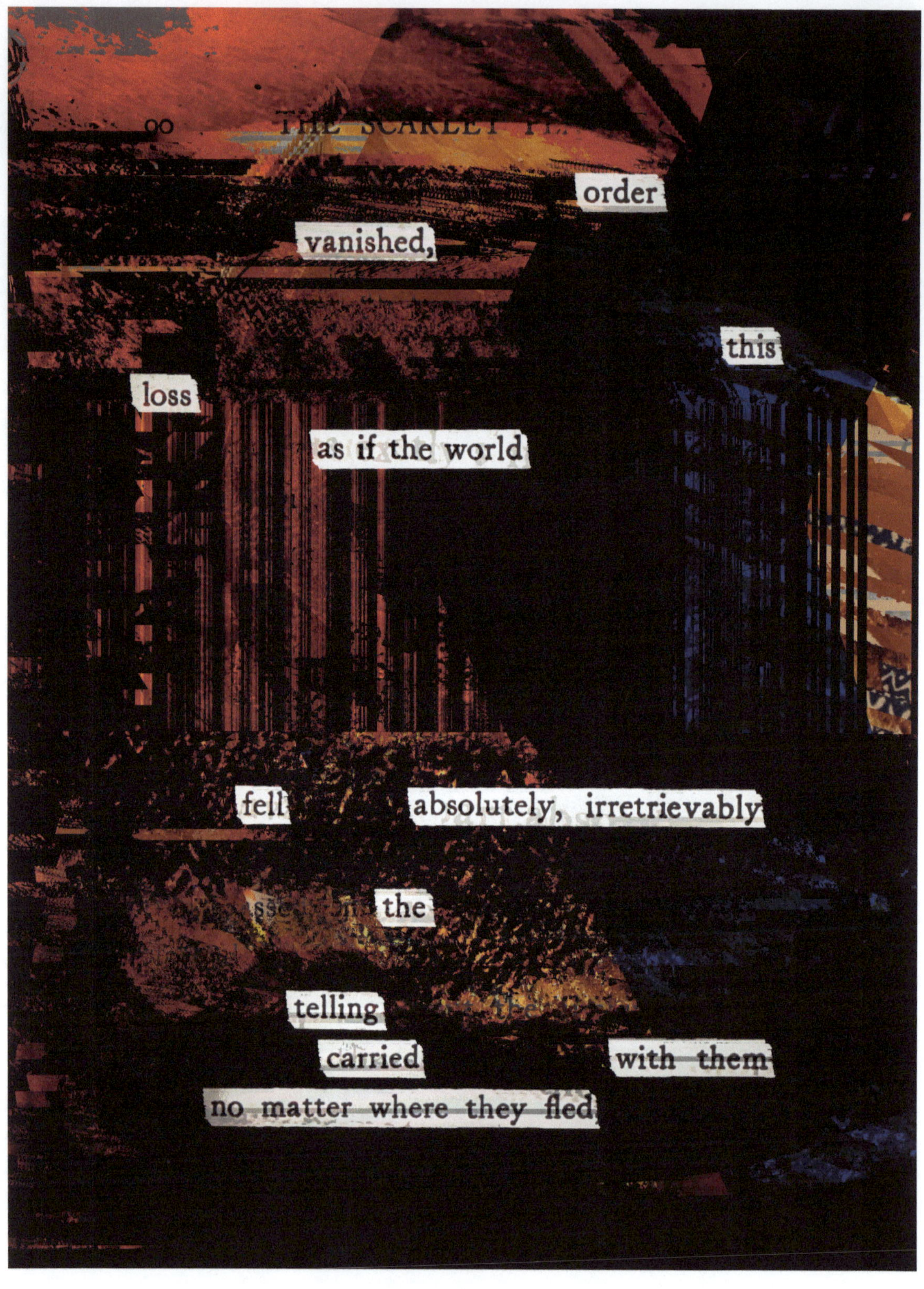
order
vanished,
this
loss
as if the world
fell   absolutely, irretrievably
the
telling
carried   with them
no matter where they fled

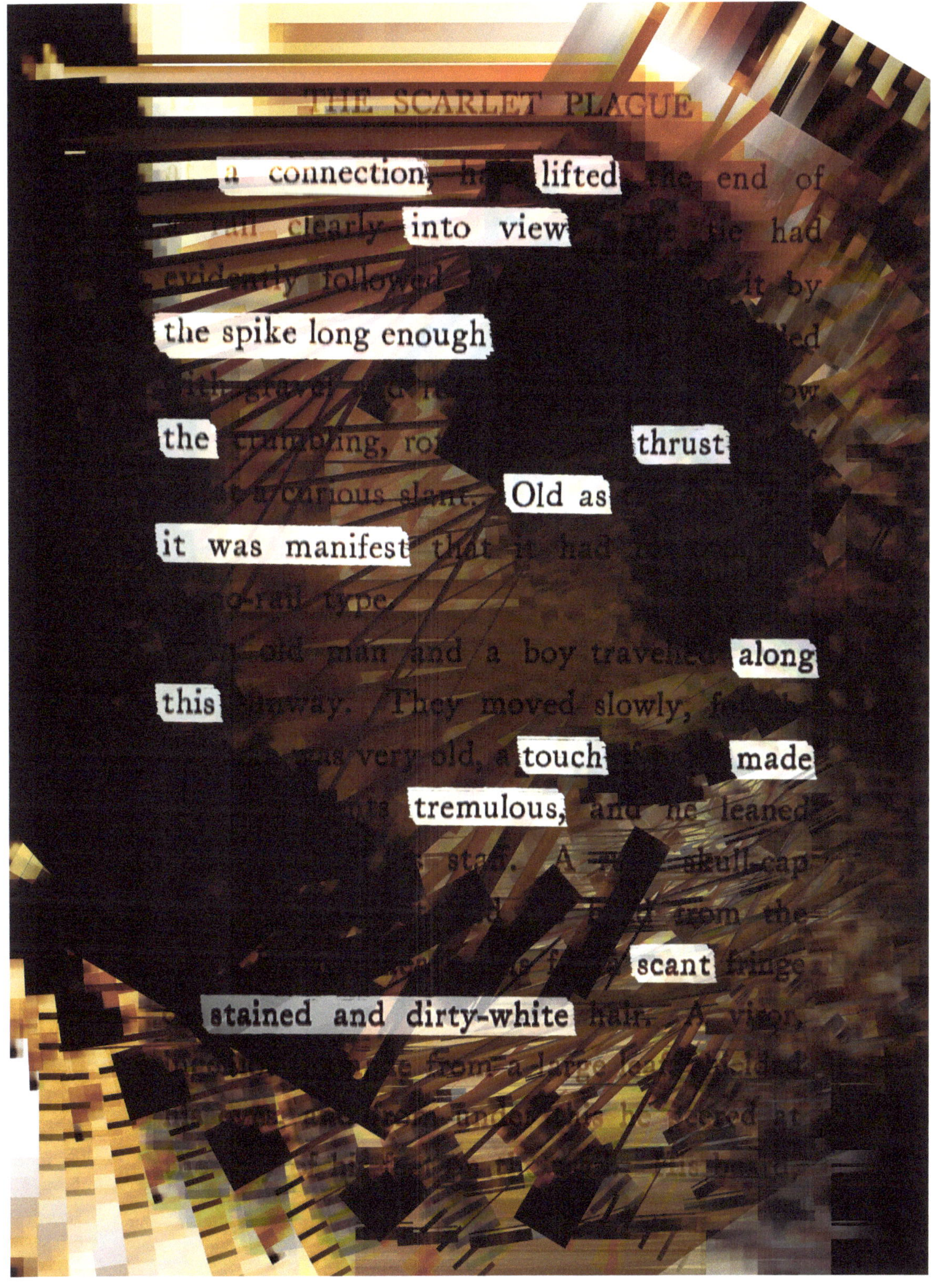

THE SCARLET PLAGUE
a connection   lifted   the end of
                  into view
the spike long enough
the   thrust
                        Old as
it was manifest
                                                        along
this
                              touch   made
                tremulous,
                                              scant
stained and dirty-white

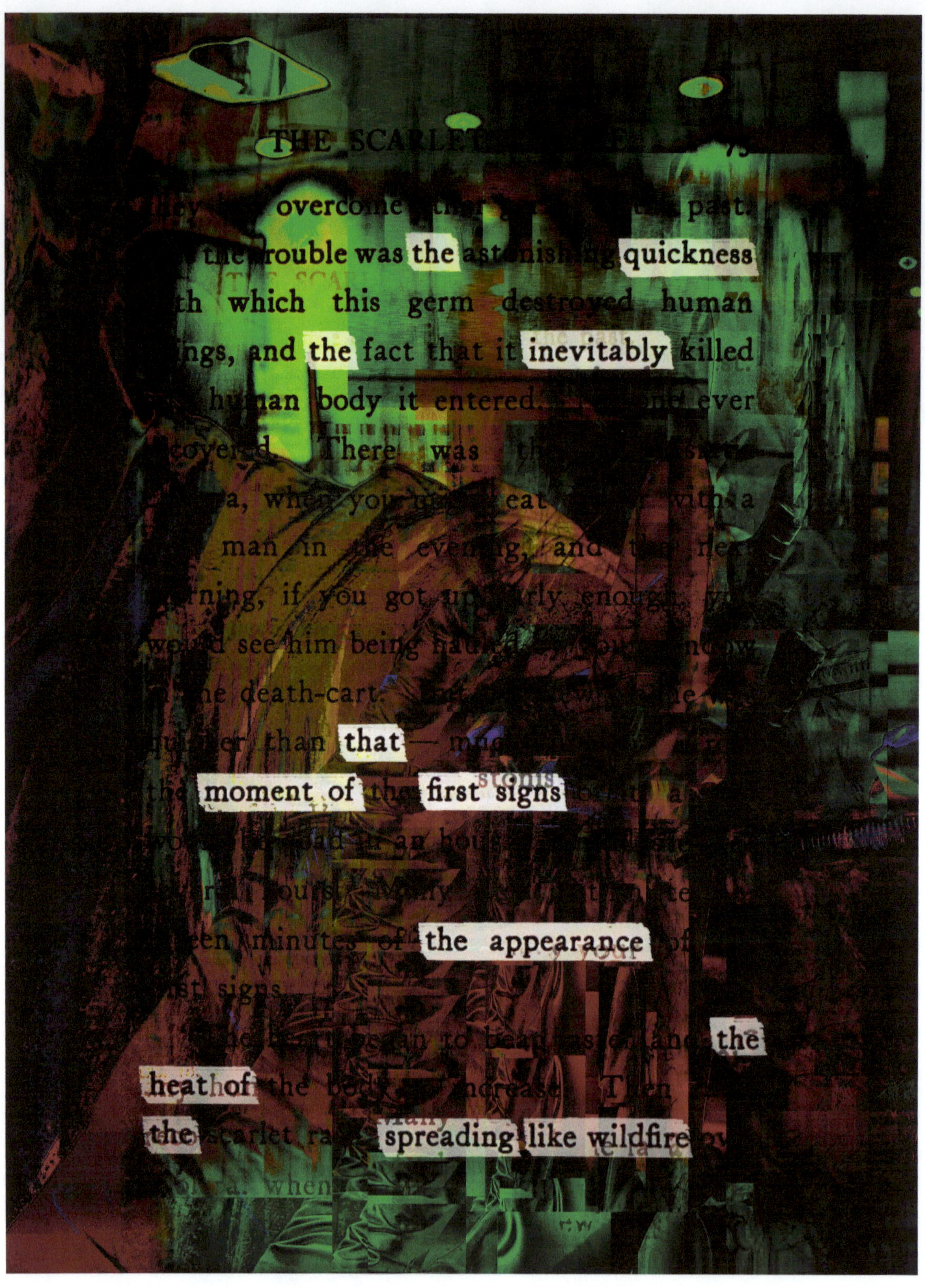
THE SCARLET
overcome
the trouble was the astonishing quickness
which this germ destroyed human
and the fact that it inevitably killed
human body it entered
There was
man in the evening
if you got up early enough
see him being
death-cart
that
the moment of the first signs
the appearance
the
heath of
the scarlet rash spreading like wildfire

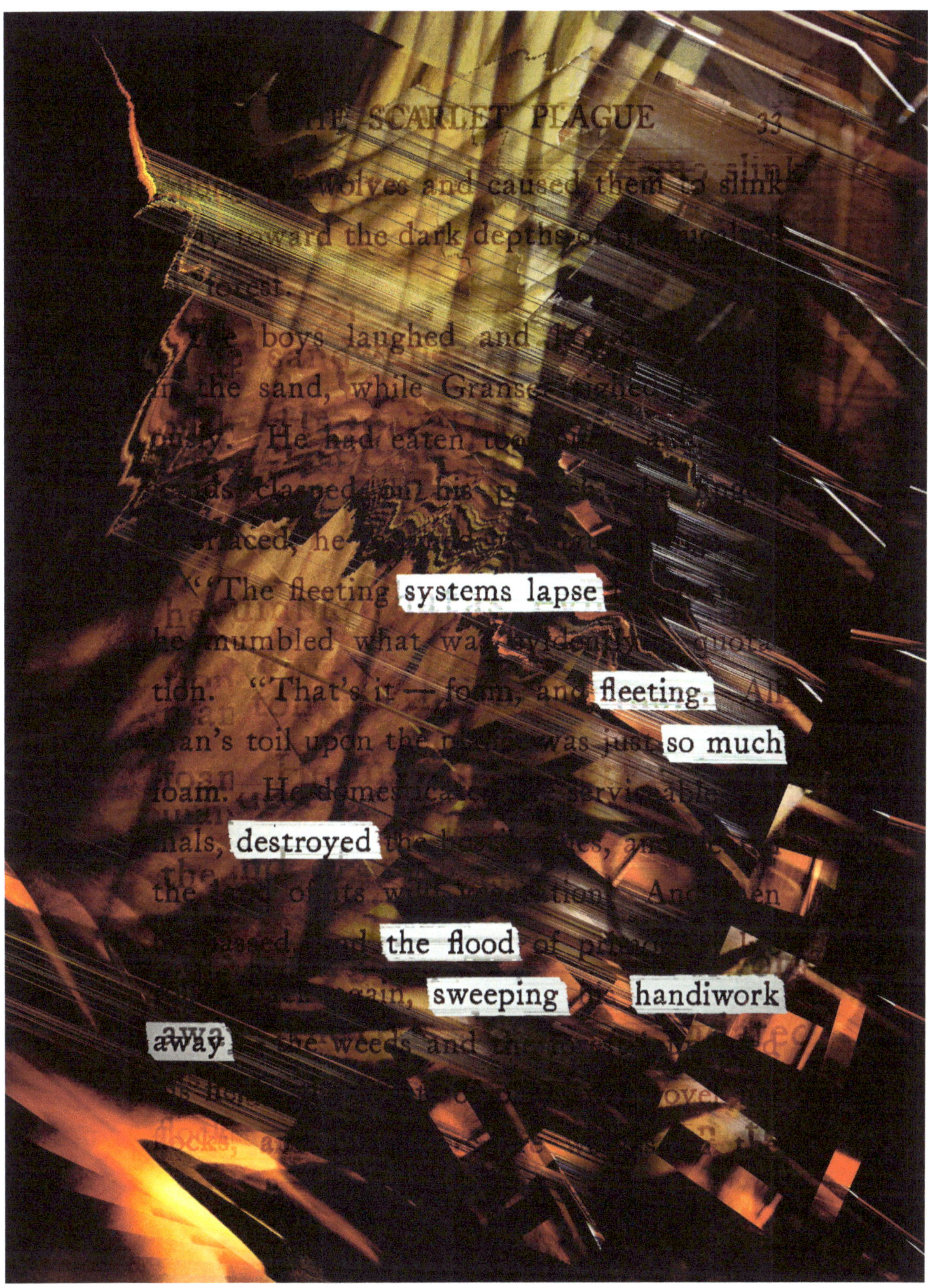
The fleeting systems lapse
fleeting
so much
destroyed
the flood of
sweeping handiwork
away

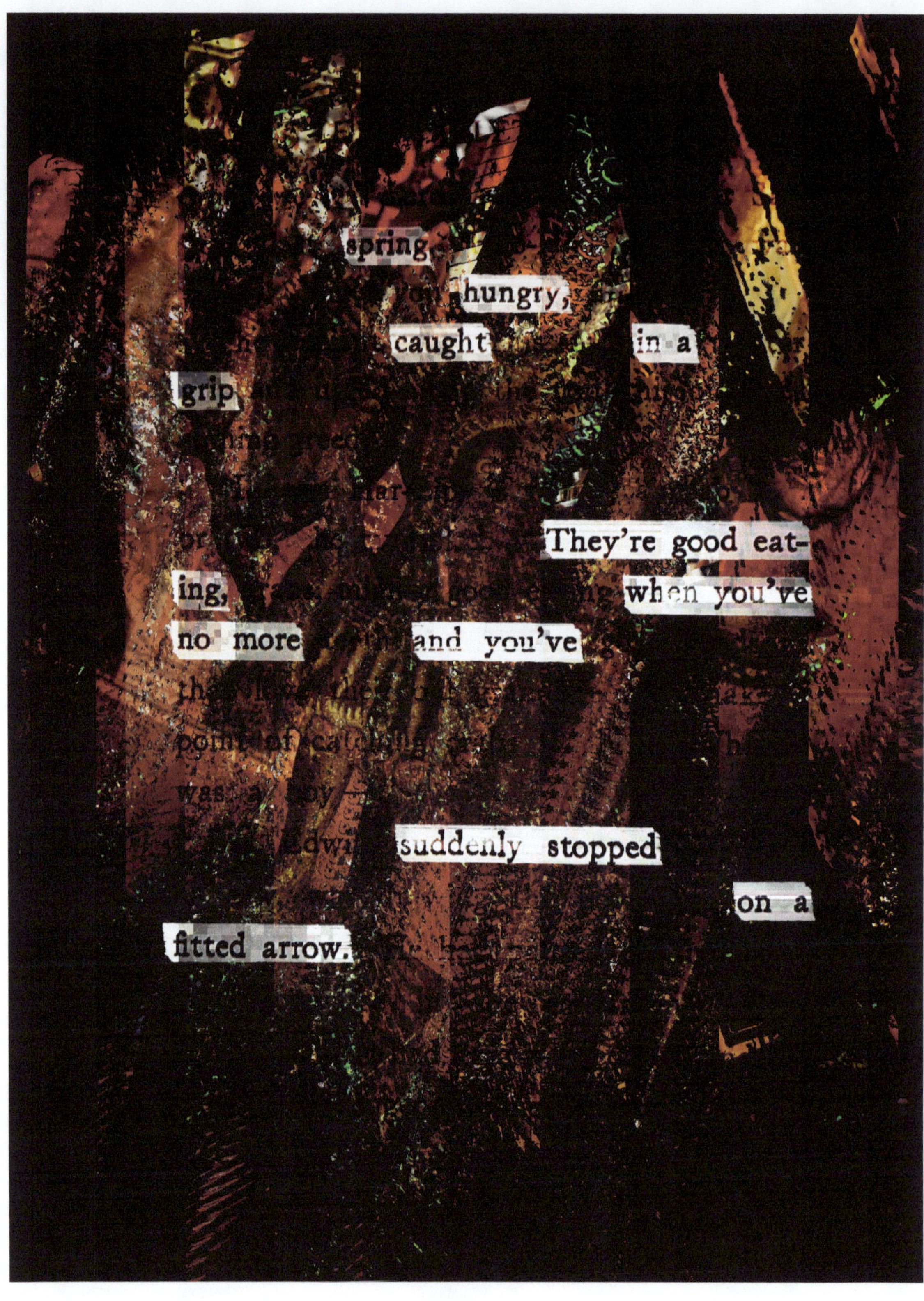
spring
hungry,
caught in a
grip
They're good eat-
ing, when you've
no more and you've
suddenly stopped
on a
fitted arrow.

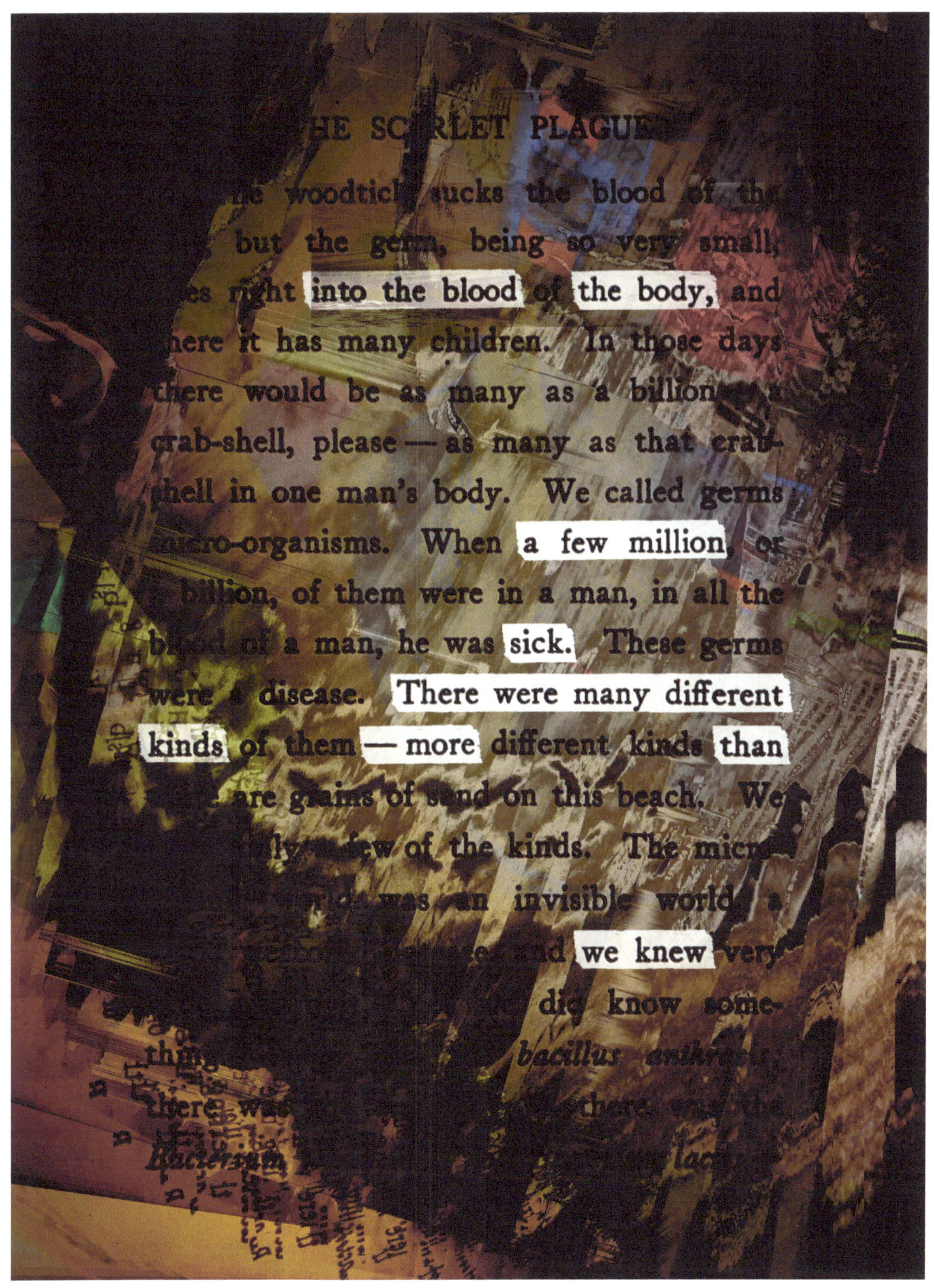
THE SCARLET PLAGUE
he woodtick sucks the blood of the
but the germ, being so very small,
right into the blood of the body, and
here it has many children. In those days
there would be as many as a billion
crab-shell, please — as many as that crab-
shell in one man's body. We called germs
micro-organisms. When a few million, or
billion, of them were in a man, in all the
blood of a man, he was sick. These germs
were a disease. There were many different
kinds of them — more different kinds than
are grains of sand on this beach. We
few of the kinds. The micro
was an invisible world, a
and we knew very
did know some-
bacillus anthracis
there was
Bacterium

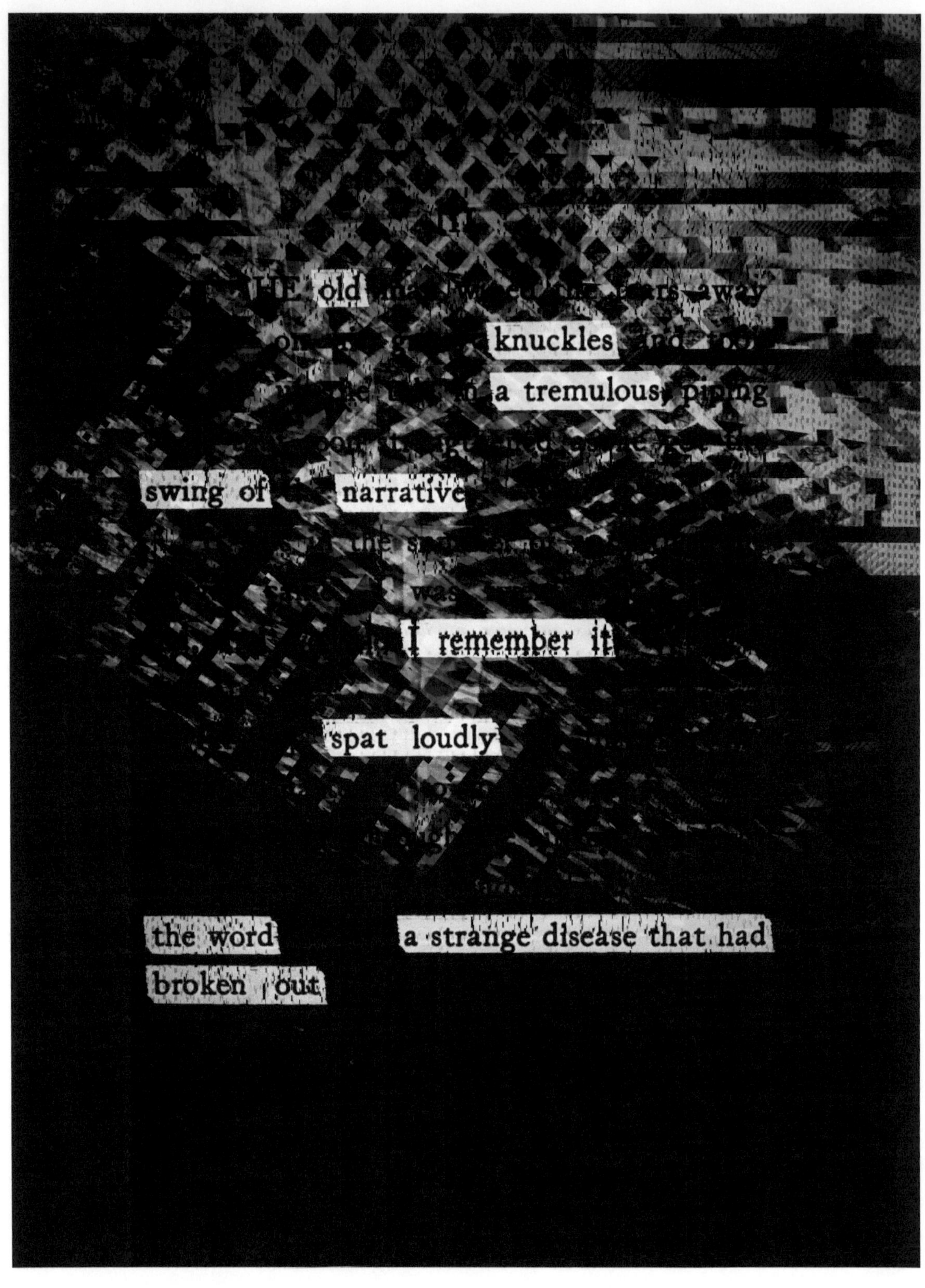

old
knuckles
a tremulous piping
swing of   narrative
I remember it
spat loudly
the word   a strange disease that had
broken out

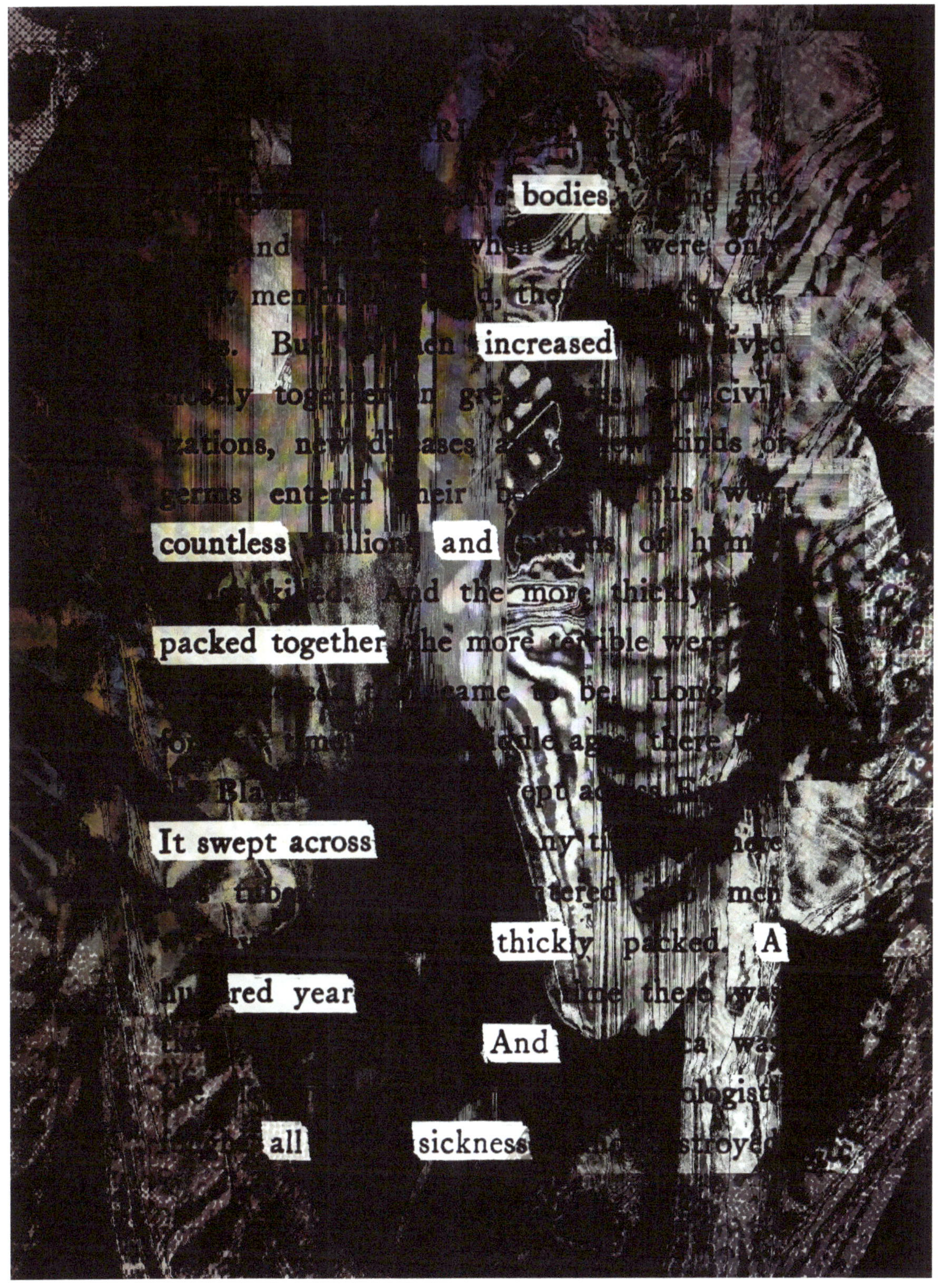
bodies
increased
countless and
packed together
It swept across
thickly packed A
red year
And
all sickness

THE SCARLET PLAGUE

...ndering about the disrespect for elders
...d the reversion to cruelty of all humans
...at fell from high culture to primitive con-
...ons.

...he tale began.

"There were very many people in the world
in those days. San Francisco alone held
four milli——"

"What is millions?" Edwin interrupted.

Granser looked at him kindly.

"I know you cannot count beyond ten,
so I will tell you. Hold up your two hands.
On both of them you have altogether ten
fingers and thumbs. Very well. I now take
this grain of sand — you hold it, Hoo-Hoo."
He dropped the grain of sand into the lad's
palm and went on. "Now that grain of sand
... the ten fingers of Edwin. I add
another grain. That's ten more fingers.
And I add another, and another, and another,

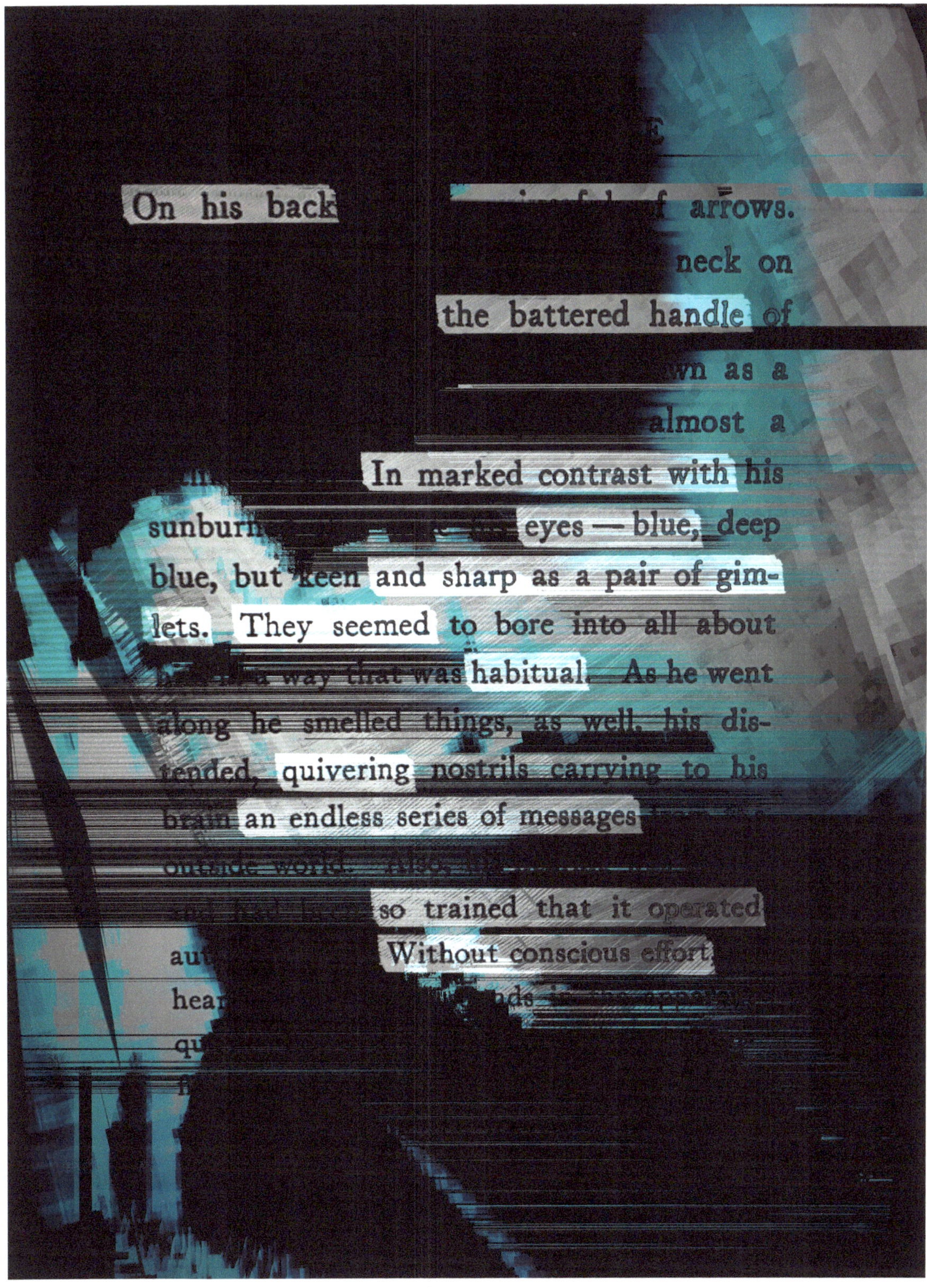
On his back
arrows.
neck on
the battered handle of
wn as a
almost a
In marked contrast with his
sunburn eyes — blue, deep
blue, but keen and sharp as a pair of gim-
lets. They seemed to bore into all about
way that was habitual. As he went
along he smelled things, as well, his dis-
tended, quivering nostrils carrying to his
brain an endless series of messages
so trained that it operated
Without conscious effort.
hear ds

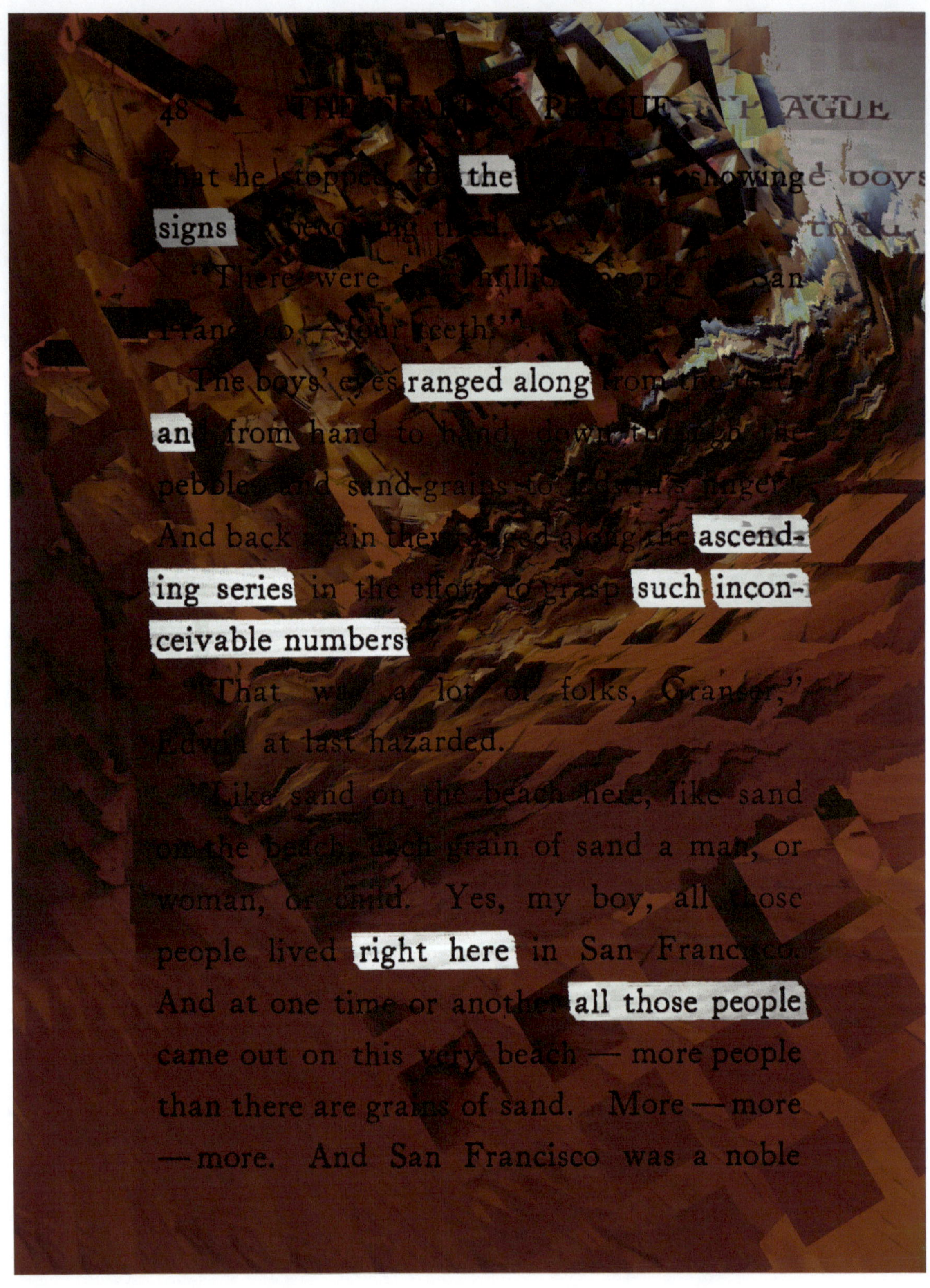
48   THE SCARLET PLAGUE   PLAGUE
that he stopped for the showing the boys
signs of becoming th...
"There were four million people in San
Francisco — four teeth...
The boys' eyes ranged along from the teeth
and from hand to hand, down through the
pebbles and sand-grains to finger...
And back again they ranged along the ascend-
ing series in the effort to grasp such incon-
ceivable numbers.
"That was a lot of folks, Granser,"
Edwin at last hazarded.
"Like sand on the beach here, like sand
on the beach, each grain of sand a man, or
woman, or child. Yes, my boy, all those
people lived right here in San Francisco.
And at one time or another all those people
came out on this very beach — more people
than there are grains of sand. More — more
— more. And San Francisco was a noble

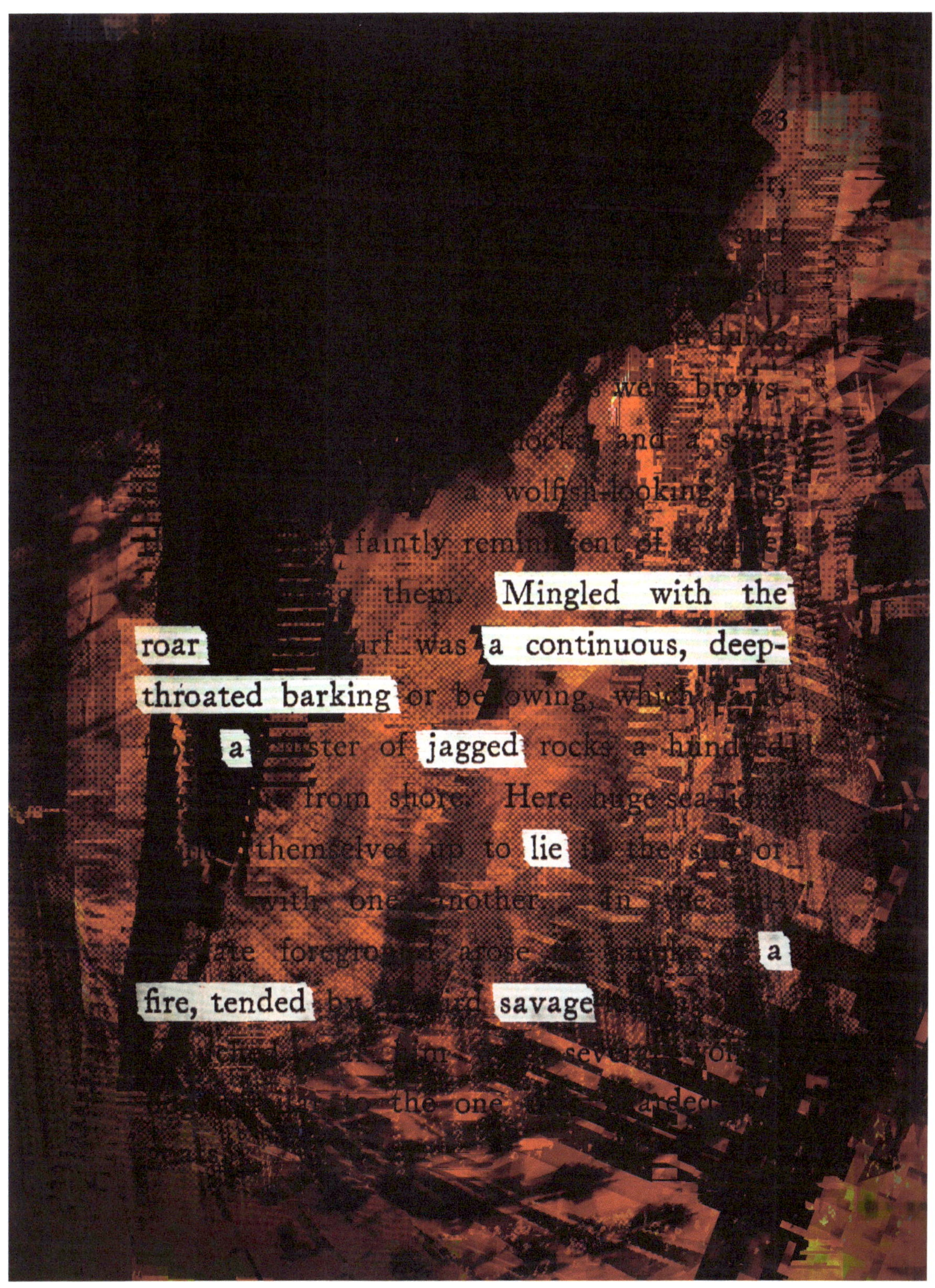
Mingled with the
roar a continuous, deep-
throated barking
a jagged
lie
a
fire, tended by savage

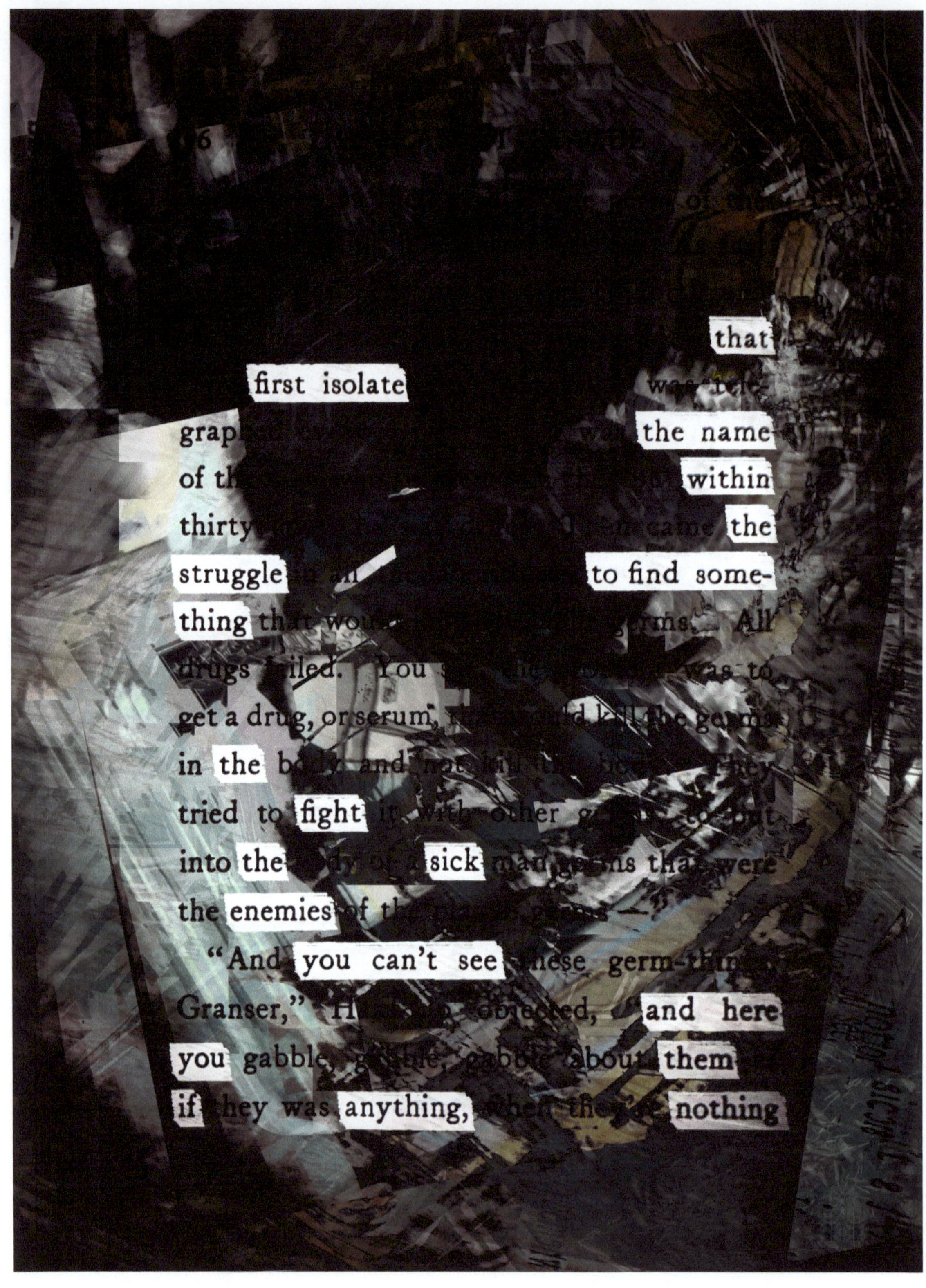
that
first isolate
the name
graph
within
of th
thirty
came the
struggle
to find some-
thing that
germs. All
drugs failed. You
was to
get a drug, or serum,
kill the germs
in the body and not kill the
they
tried to fight it with other germs to put
into the body of a sick man germs that were
the enemies of the
"And you can't see these germ-things,
Granser," objected, and here
you gabble, gabble, gabble about them
if they was anything, when they are nothing

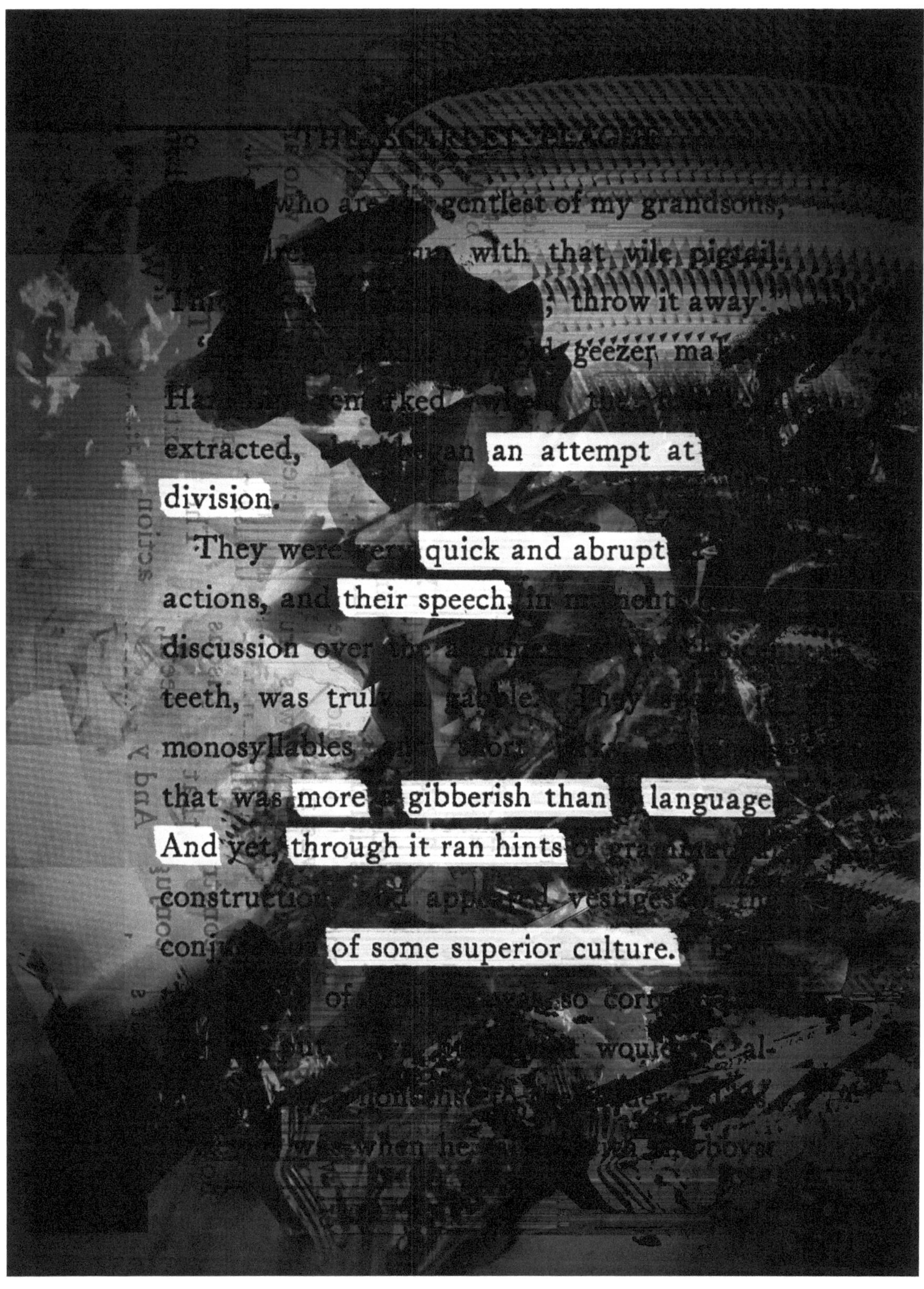
an attempt at
division.
quick and abrupt
their speech,
that was more gibberish than language
And yet, through it ran hints
of some superior culture.

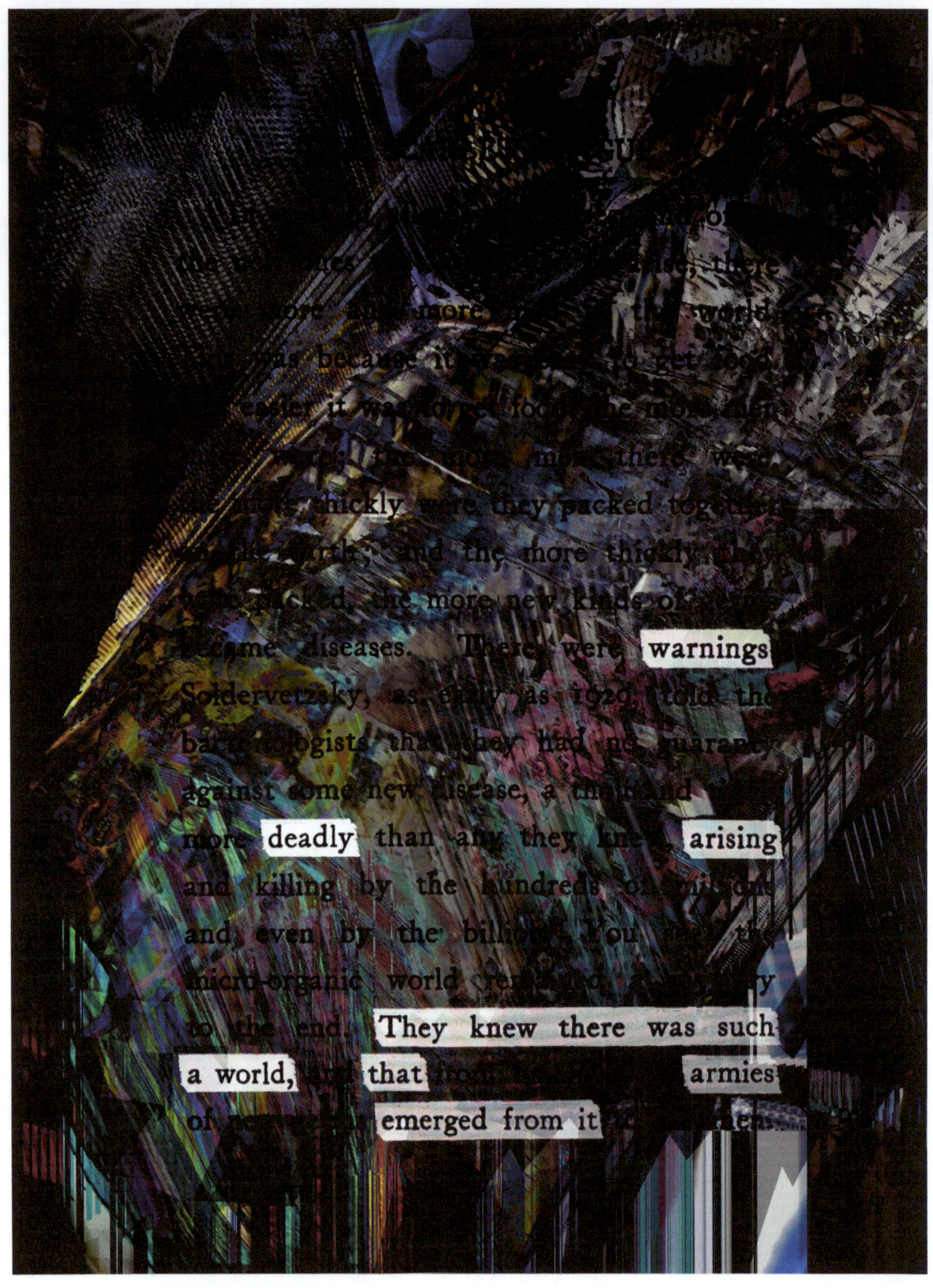
warnings
deadly than any they knew, arising
They knew there was such
a world, and that
armies
emerged from it

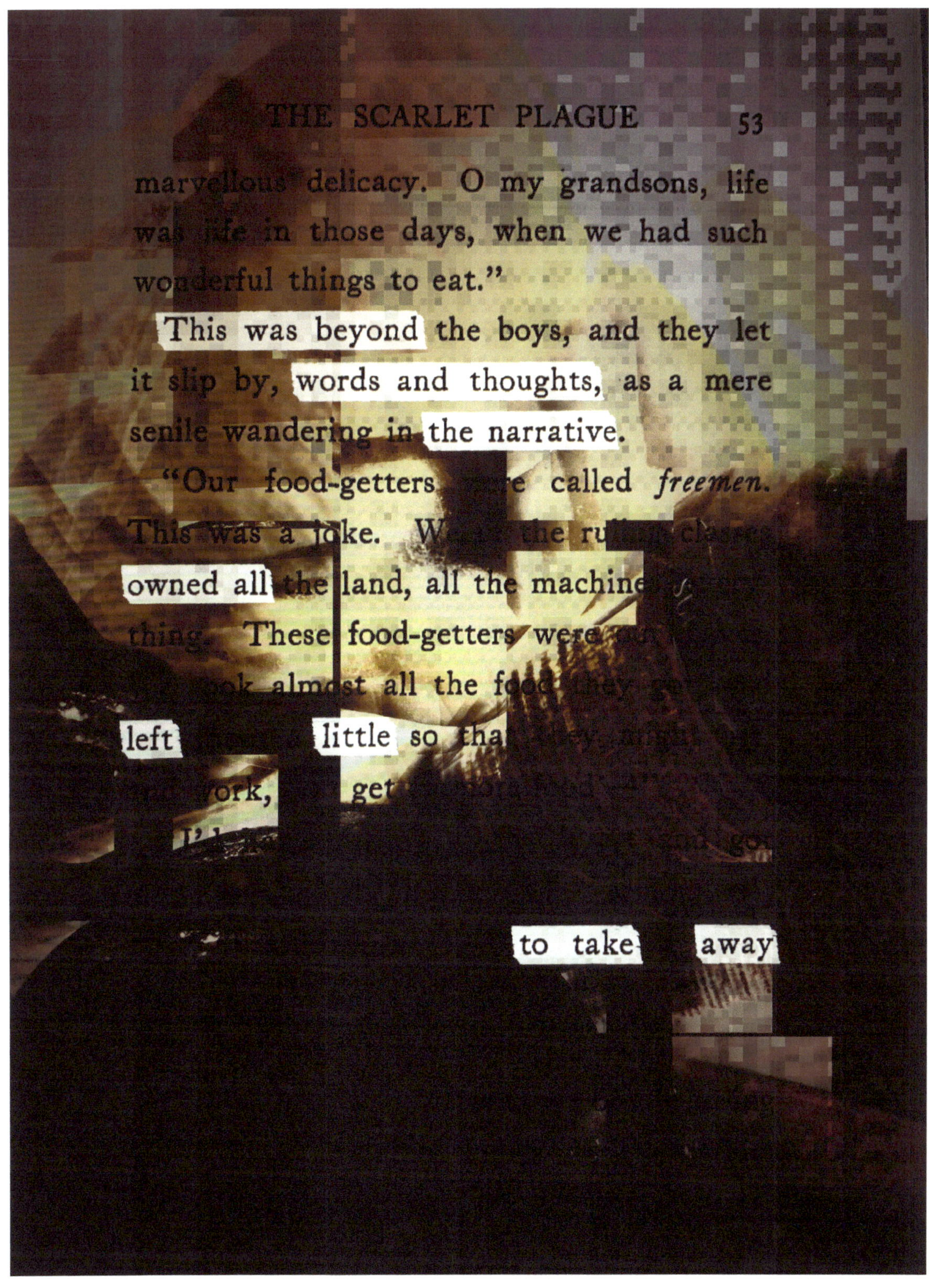
THE SCARLET PLAGUE   53
marvellous delicacy. O my grandsons, life
was life in those days, when we had such
wonderful things to eat."
This was beyond the boys, and they let
it slip by, words and thoughts, as a mere
senile wandering in the narrative.
"Our food-getters were called freemen.
This was a joke. When the ruling classes
owned all the land, all the machines, every-
thing. These food-getters were
almost all the food they
left   little so that they
work,   get more food
I'
to take   away

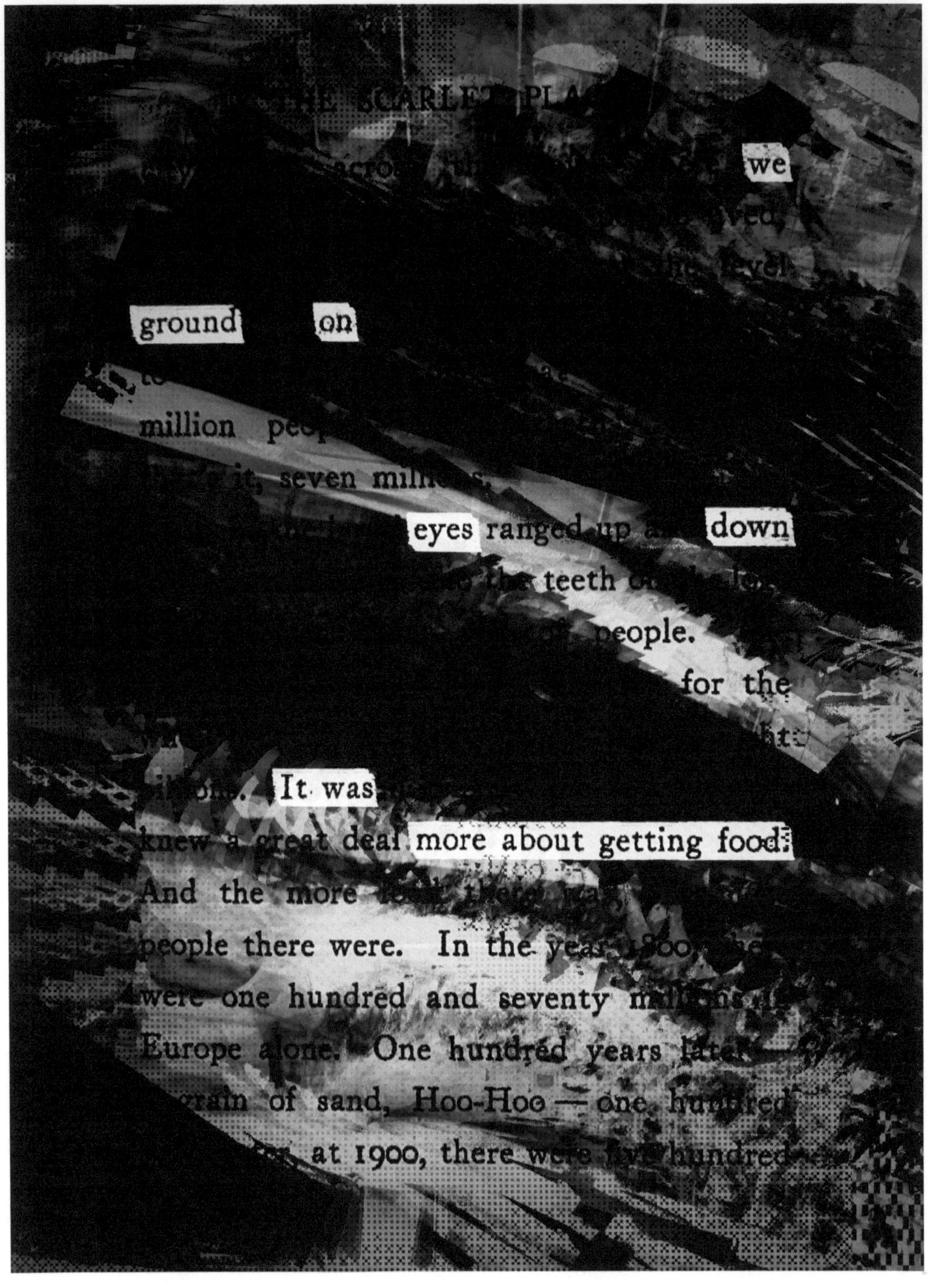
we
ground   on
million peo
it, seven mill
eyes ranged up a   down
the teeth
people.
for the
It was
knew a great deal more about getting food.
And the more
people there were. In the year 1800
were one hundred and seventy mill
Europe alone. One hundred years late
grain of sand, Hoo-Hoo — one hundred
at 1900, there were five hundred

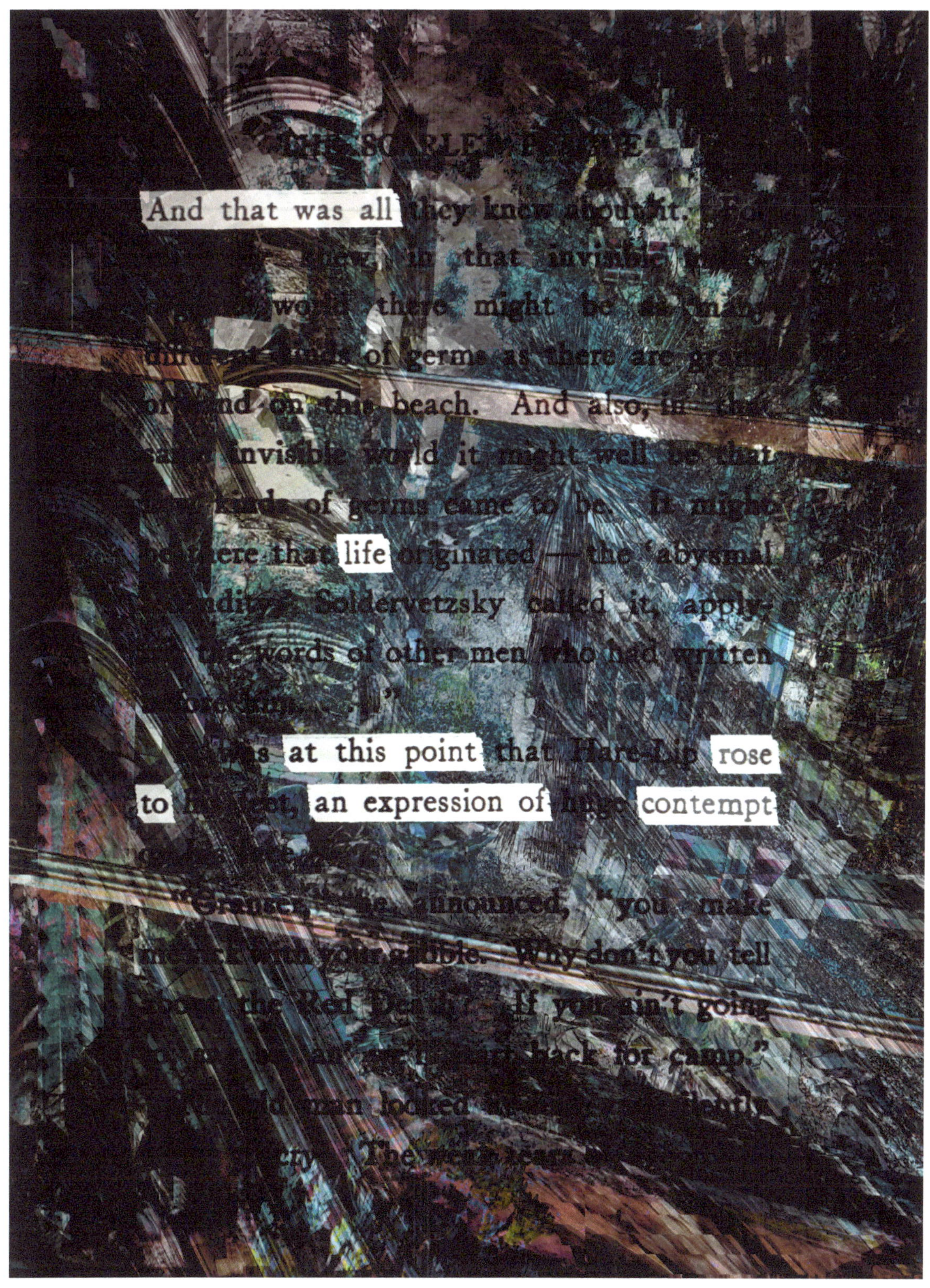
THE SCARLET PLAGUE
And that was all they knew about it. ... in that invisible ... world there might be ... different kinds of germs as there are grains of sand on the beach. And also, in that ... invisible world it might well be that ... kinds of germs came to be. It might ... be there that life originated — the 'abysmal ... fecundity' Soldervetzsky called it, apply- ... the words of other men who had written ...
...s at this point that Hare-Lip rose to his feet, an expression of huge contempt ...
"Granser," he announced, "you make me ... with your gabble. Why don't you tell ... about the Red Death? ... If you ain't going ... back for camp." ... old man looked ... The ...

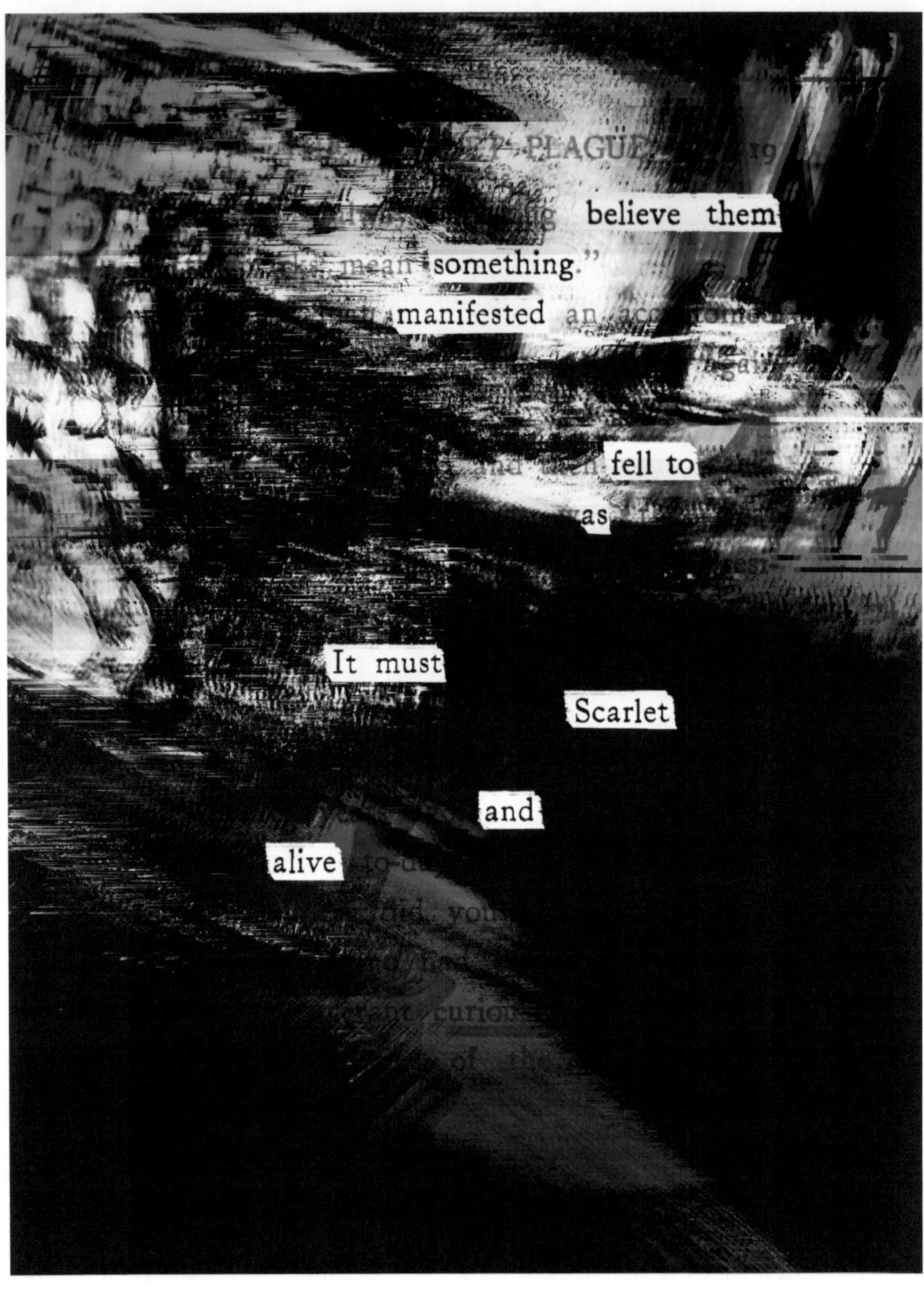
believe them
mean "something."
manifested an
fell to
It must
Scarlet
and
alive

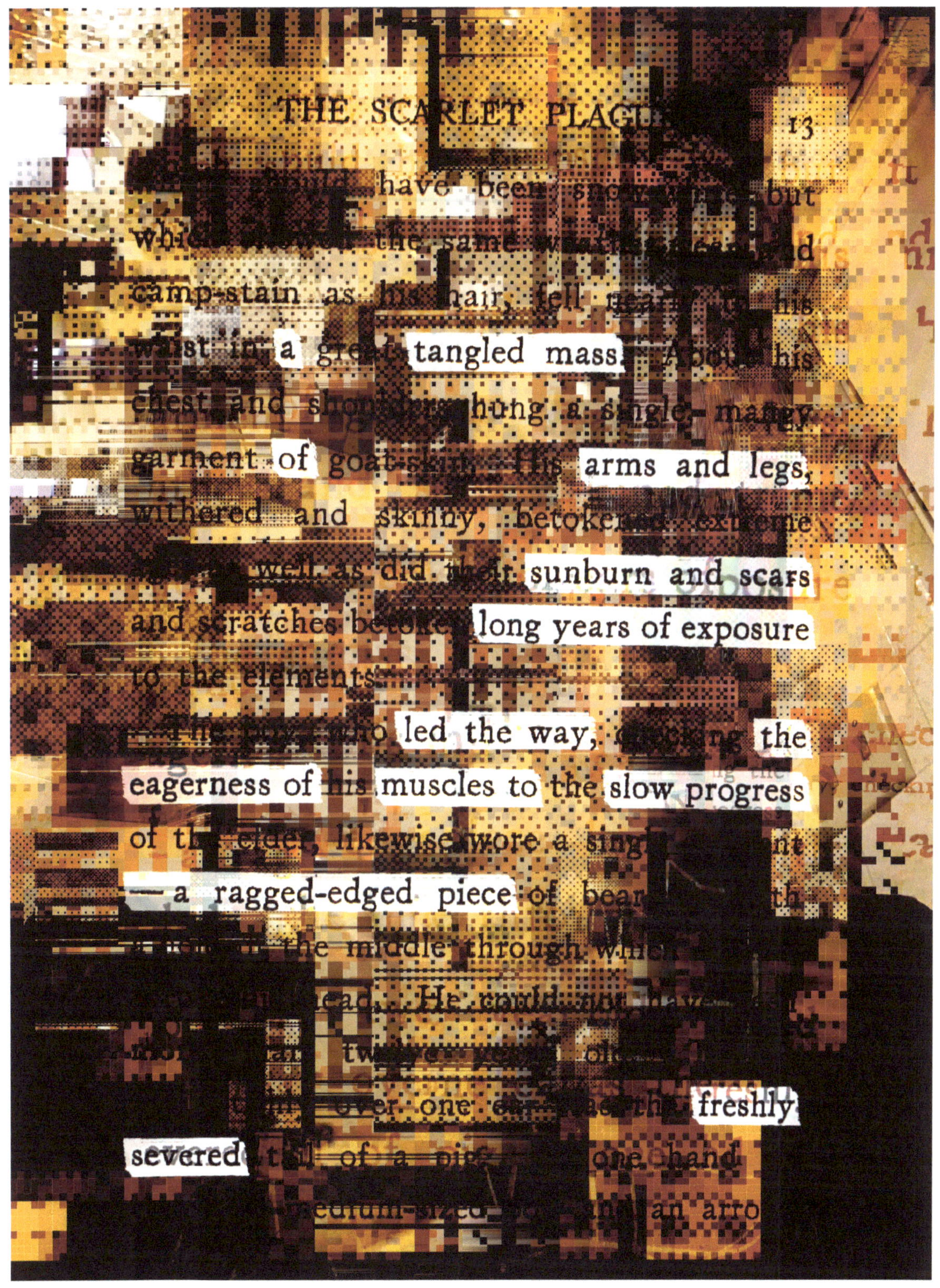
THE SCARLET PLAGUE   13
have been
which the same
camp-stain as his hair, fell near to his
waist in a great tangled mass. About his
chest and shoulders hung a single matted
garment of goat-skin. His arms and legs,
withered and skinny, betokened extreme
well as did their sunburn and scars
and scratches long years of exposure
to the elements
led the way, checking the
eagerness of his muscles to the slow progress
of the elder, likewise wore a single garment
— a ragged-edged piece of bear
the middle through which
head. He could not have
twelve years old
over one freshly
severed tail of a pig   one hand
medium-sized   an arro

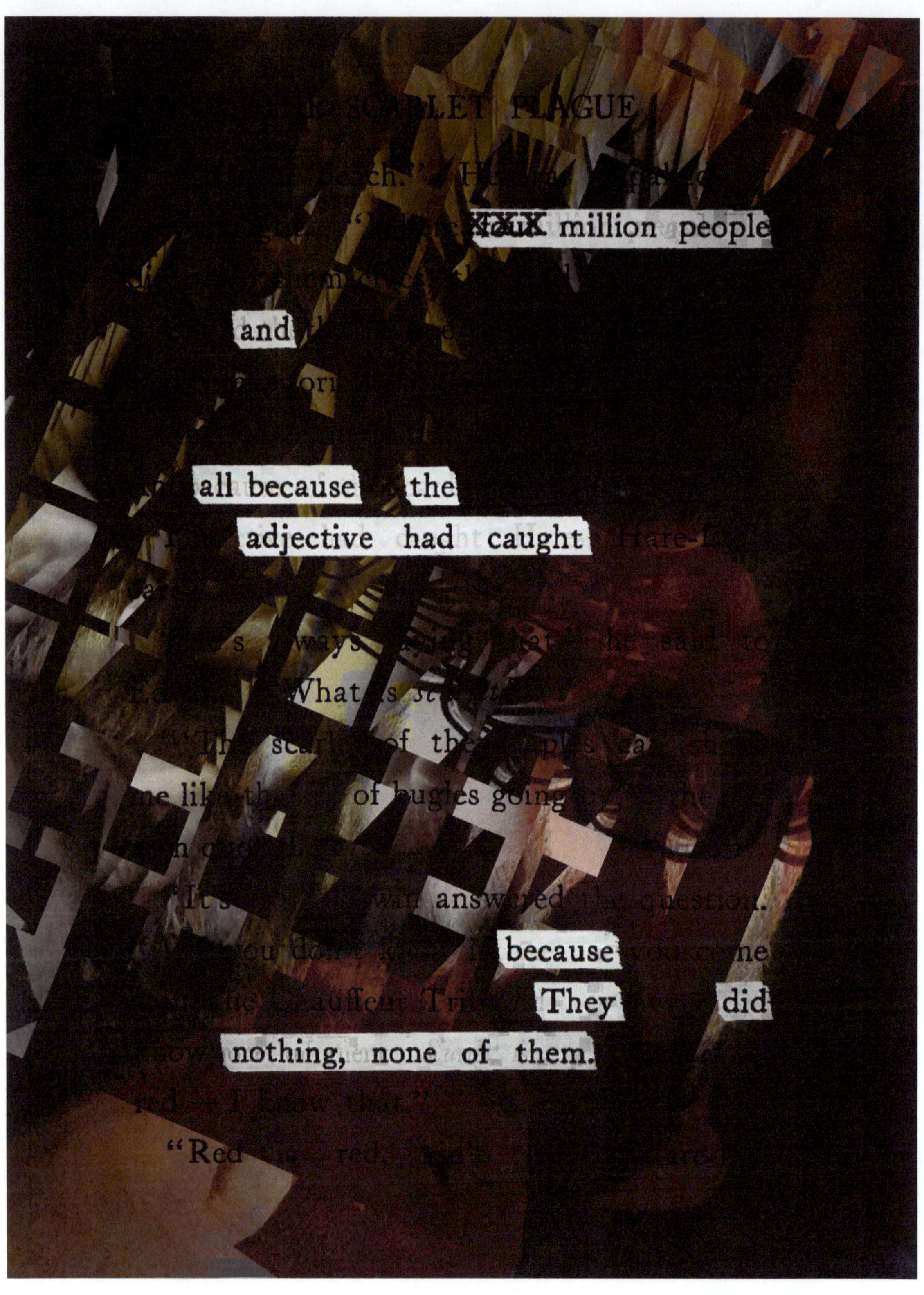
XXX million people
and
all because the
adjective had caught
because you come
They did
nothing, none of them.

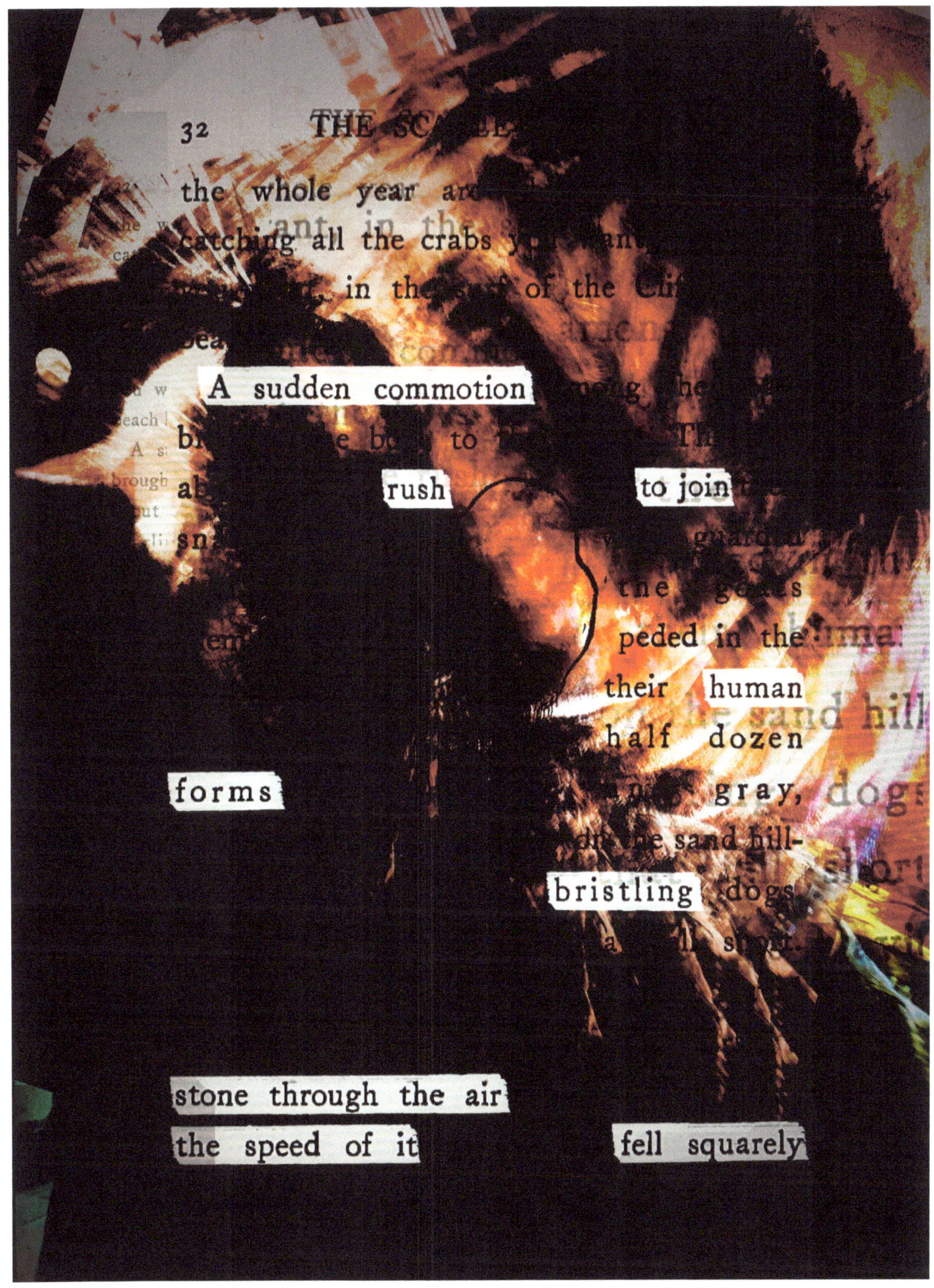

32   THE SCARLET
the whole year and
catching all the crabs you want
in the surf of the Cliff
A sudden commotion
rush   to join
the goats
peded in the human
their   human
half   dozen
forms   gray,   dogs
on the sand hill-
bristling   dogs
stone through the air
the speed of it   fell squarely

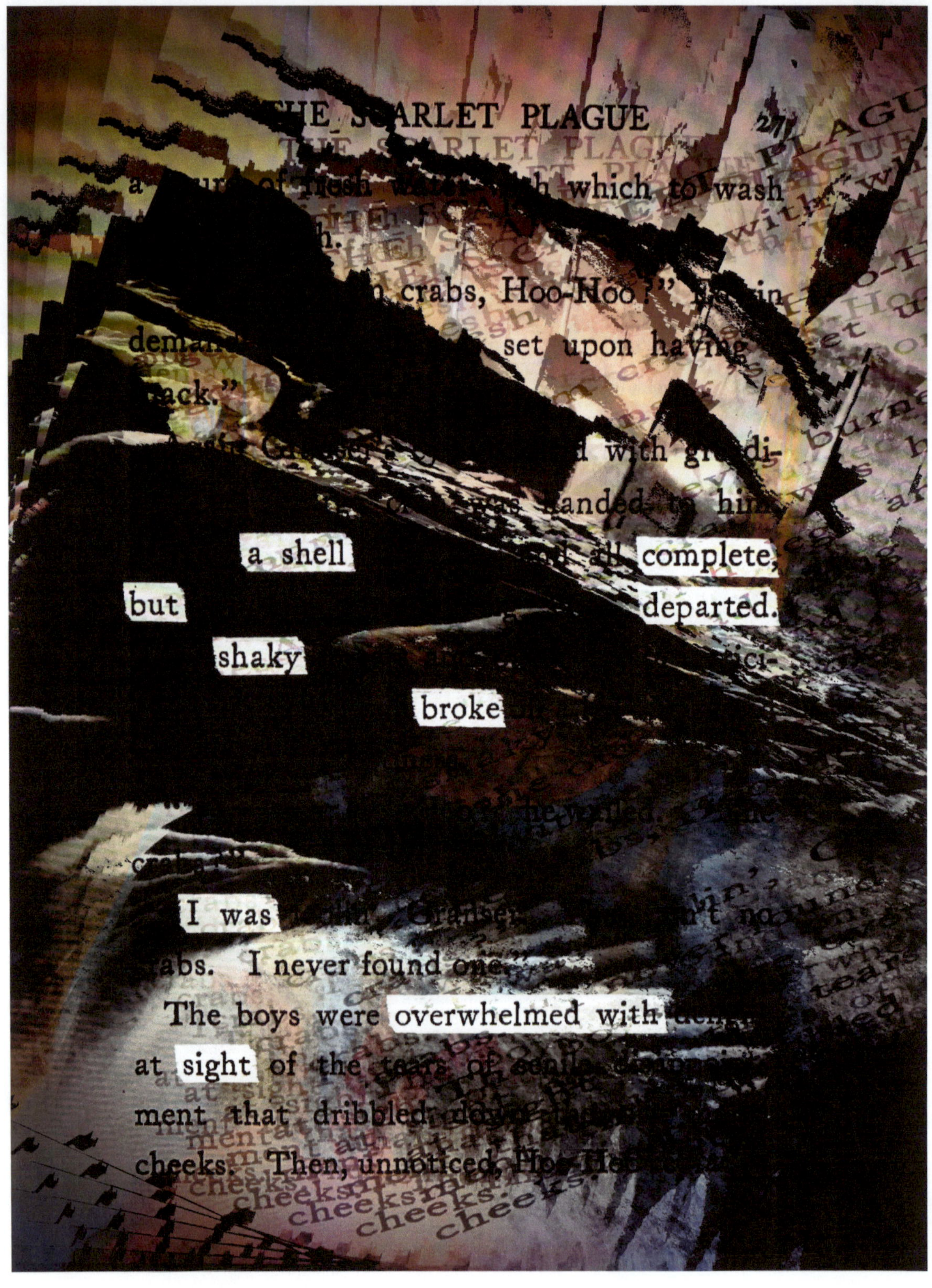
a shell
but
shaky
complete,
departed.
broke
I was
overwhelmed with
at sight

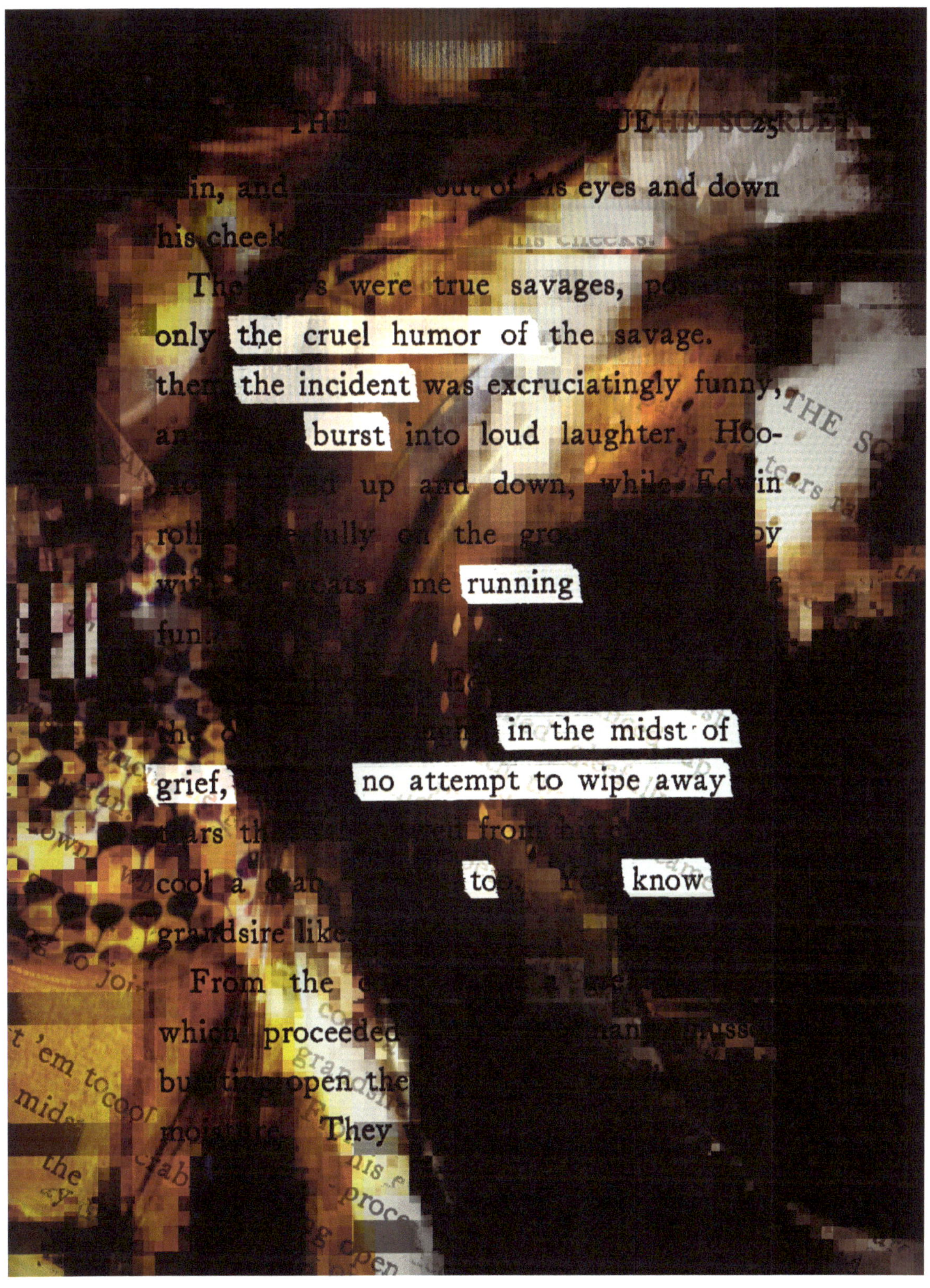
in, and out of his eyes and down
his cheek
The were true savages,
only the cruel humor of the savage.
them the incident was excruciatingly funny,
an burst into loud laughter. Hoo-
up and down, while Edwin
roll fully on the gro by
wit eats me running
fun
in the midst of
grief, no attempt to wipe away
ars th from
cool a to know
grandsire like
From the
which proceeded
bu ing open the
mo ce. They

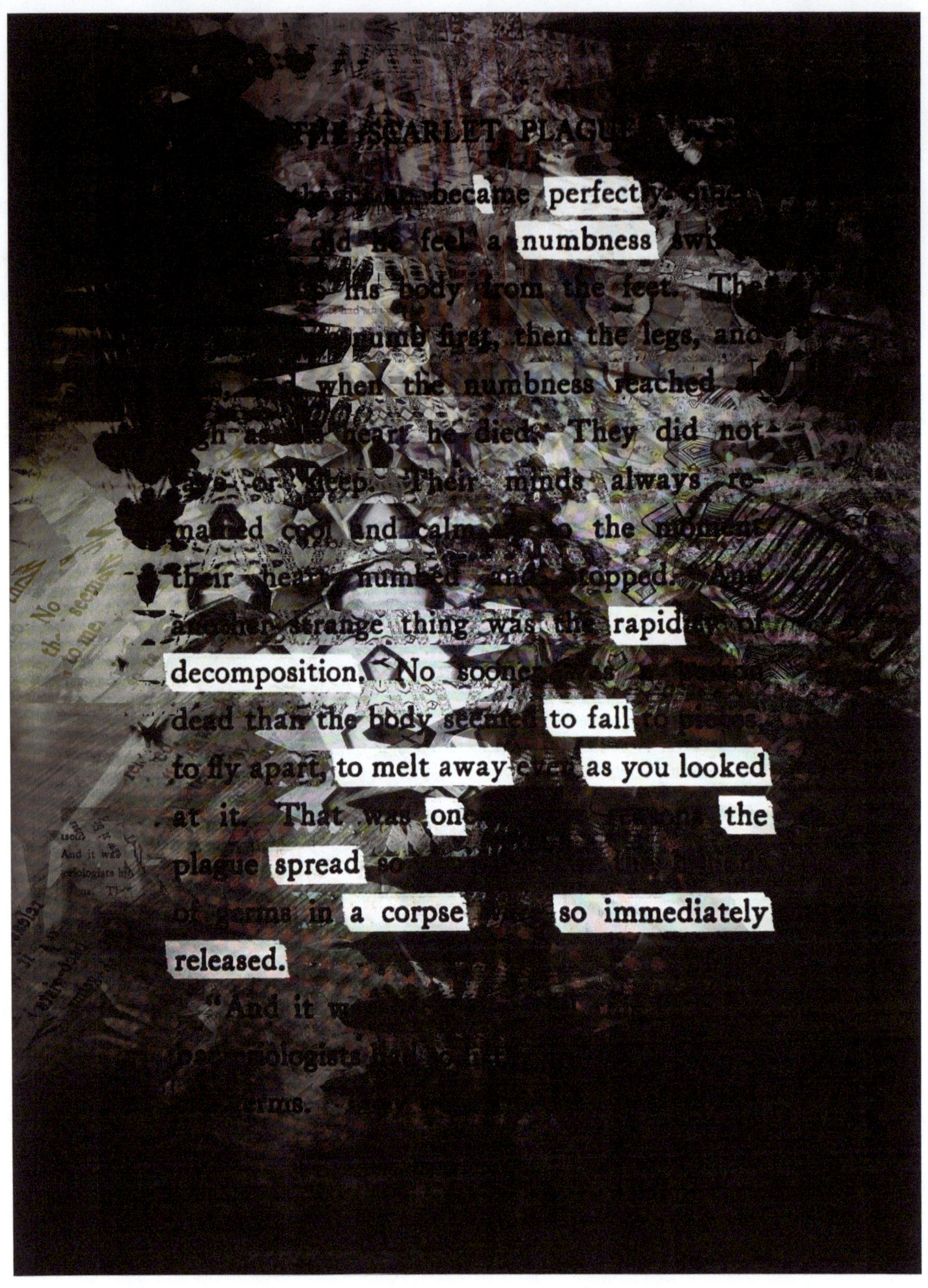
THE SCARLET PLAGUE
became perfectly
did he feel a numbness
his body from the feet. The
numb first, then the legs, and
when the numbness reached
his heart he died. They did not
or weep. Their minds always re-
mained cool and calm to the moment
their hearts numbed and stopped. And
another strange thing was the rapidity of
decomposition. No sooner was a
dead than the body seemed to fall to pieces,
to fly apart, to melt away even as you looked
at it. That was one the
plague spread so
of germs in a corpse so immediately
released.
"And it
bacteriologists
germs.

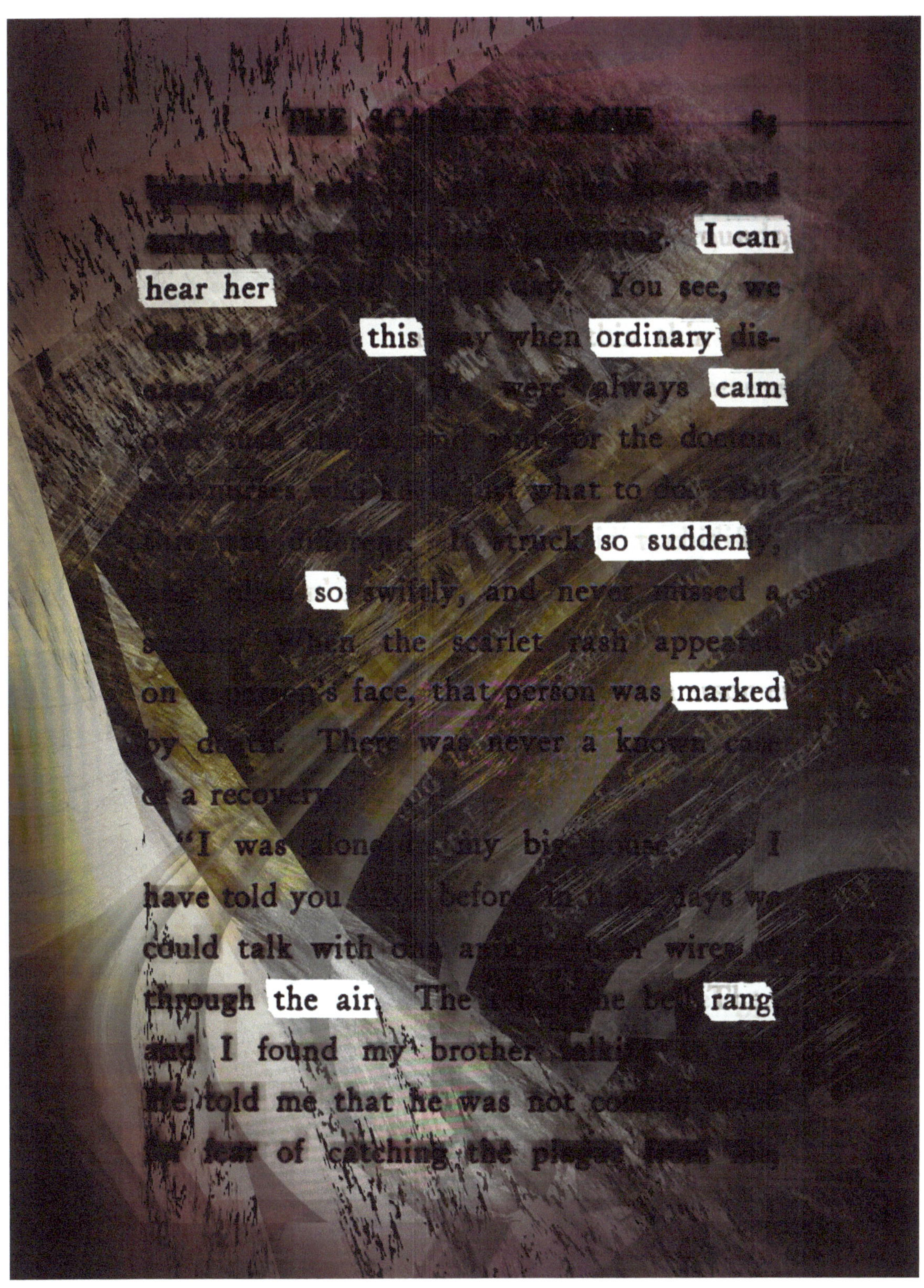
I can
hear her
this ordinary calm
so sudden
so marked
the air rang

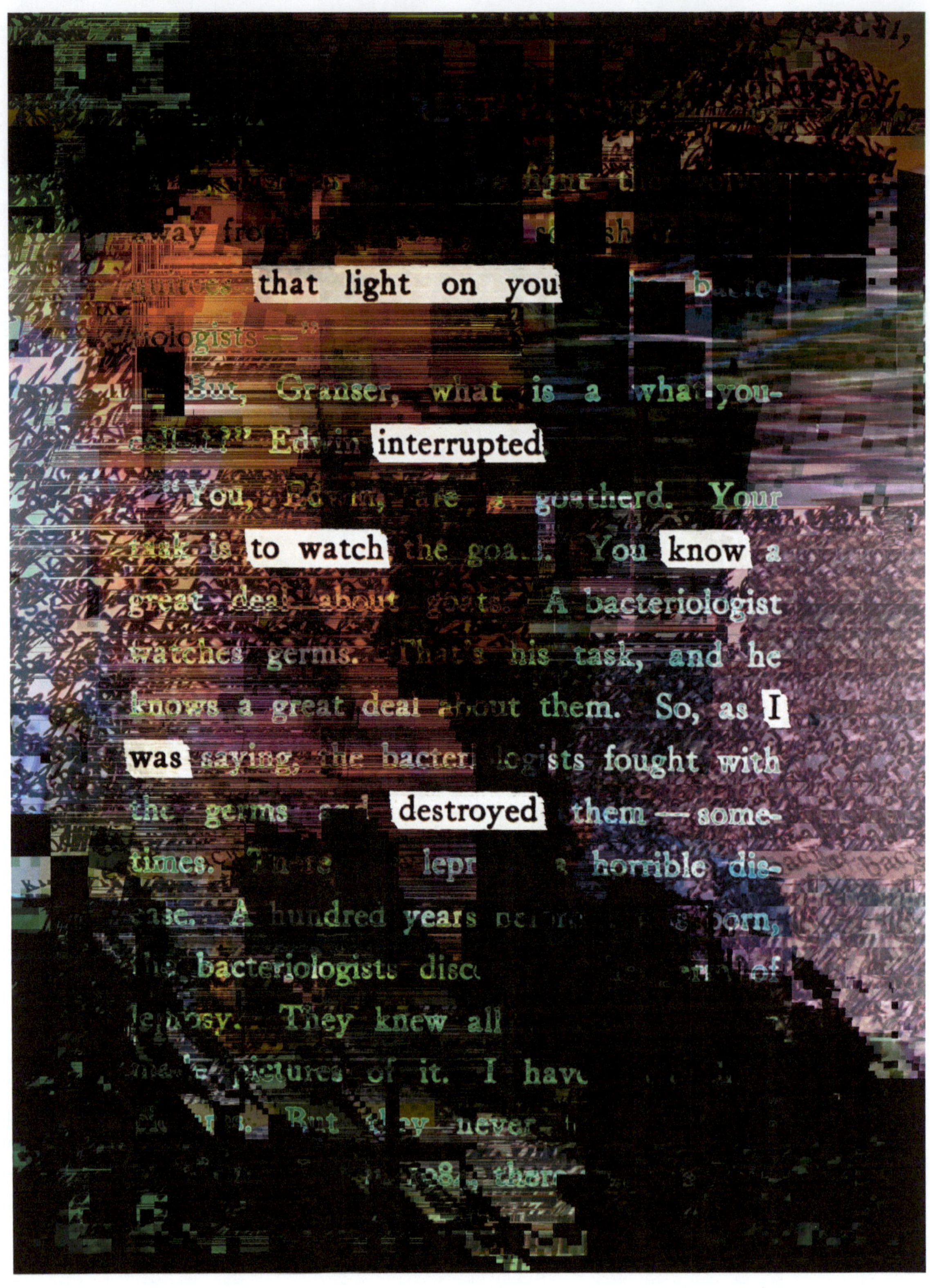
that light on you
But, Granser, what is a what-you-
Edwin interrupted
"You, Edwin, are a goatherd. Your
task is to watch the goats. You know a
great deal about goats. A bacteriologist
watches germs. That's his task, and he
knows a great deal about them. So, as I
was saying, the bacteriologists fought with
the germs and destroyed them — some-
times. There was leprosy, a horrible dis-
ease. A hundred years before you were born,
the bacteriologists discovered the germ of
leprosy. They knew all
pictures of it. I have
But they never
there

BARE FLOOR, WITH COAT HANGER

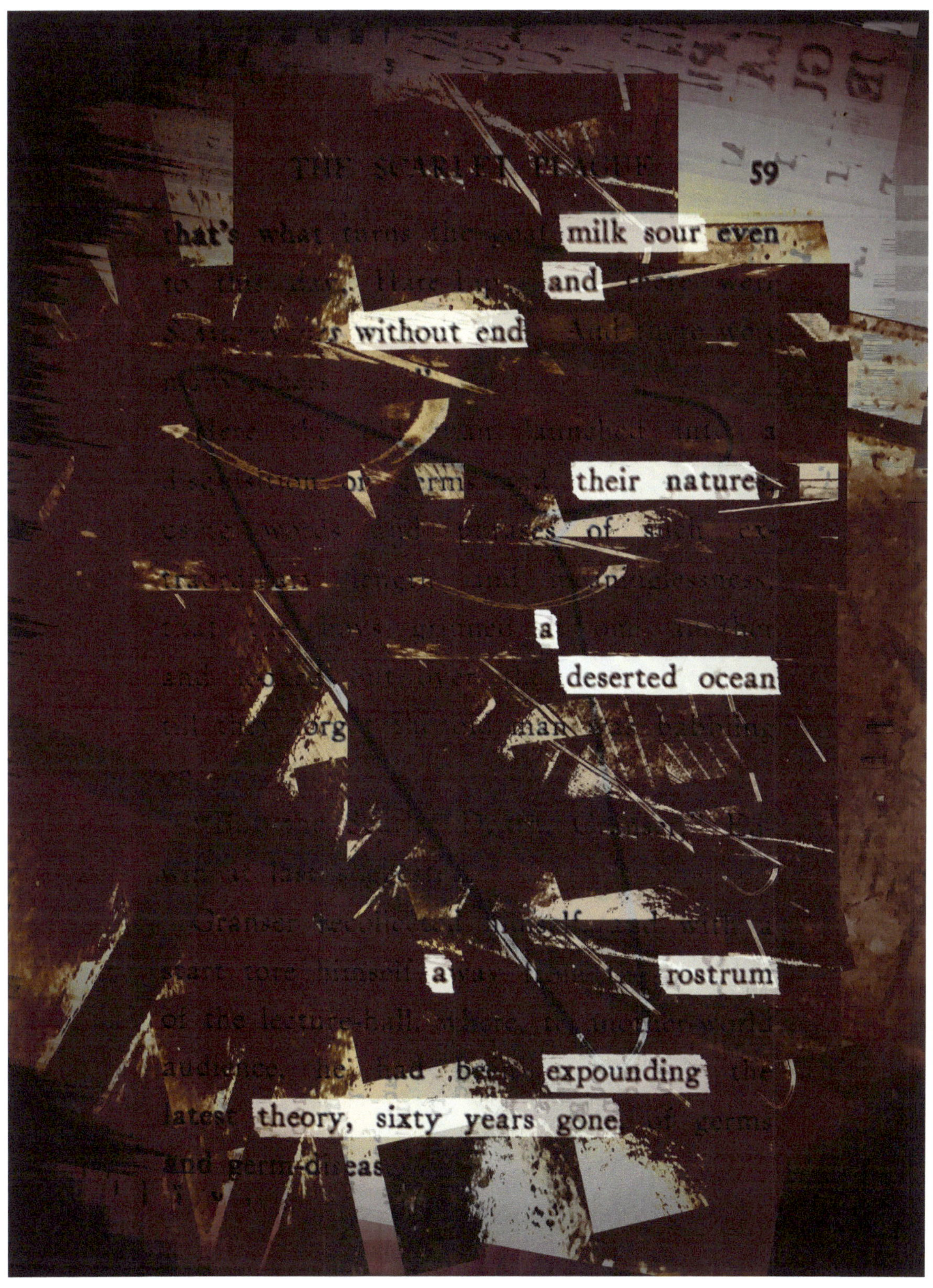

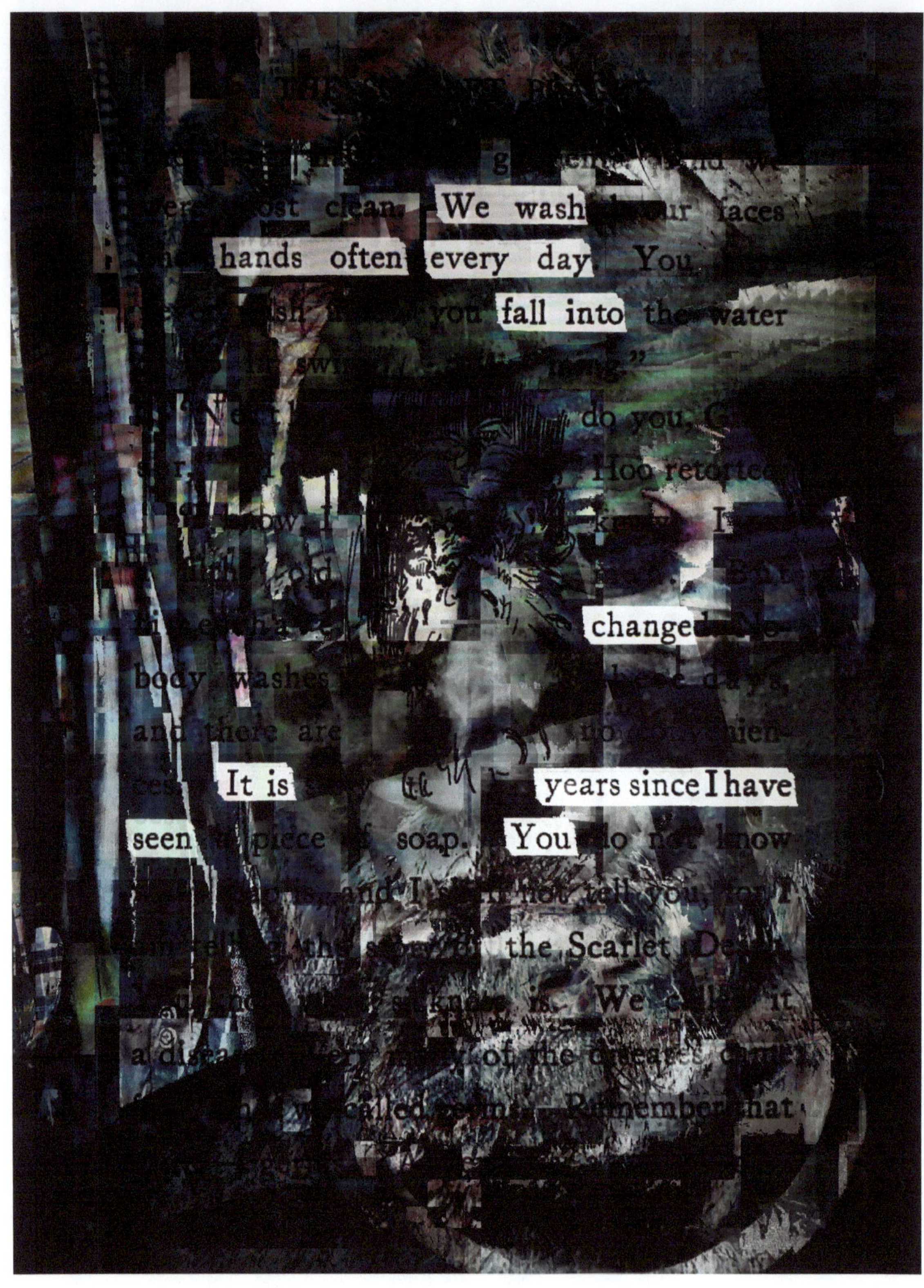
We wash our faces
hands often every day. You
you fall into the water
do you, G.
Hoo retorted
I
changed
body washes
and there are
It is
years since I have
seen a piece of soap. You do not know
the story of the Scarlet De
We call it
of the Scarlet
Remember that

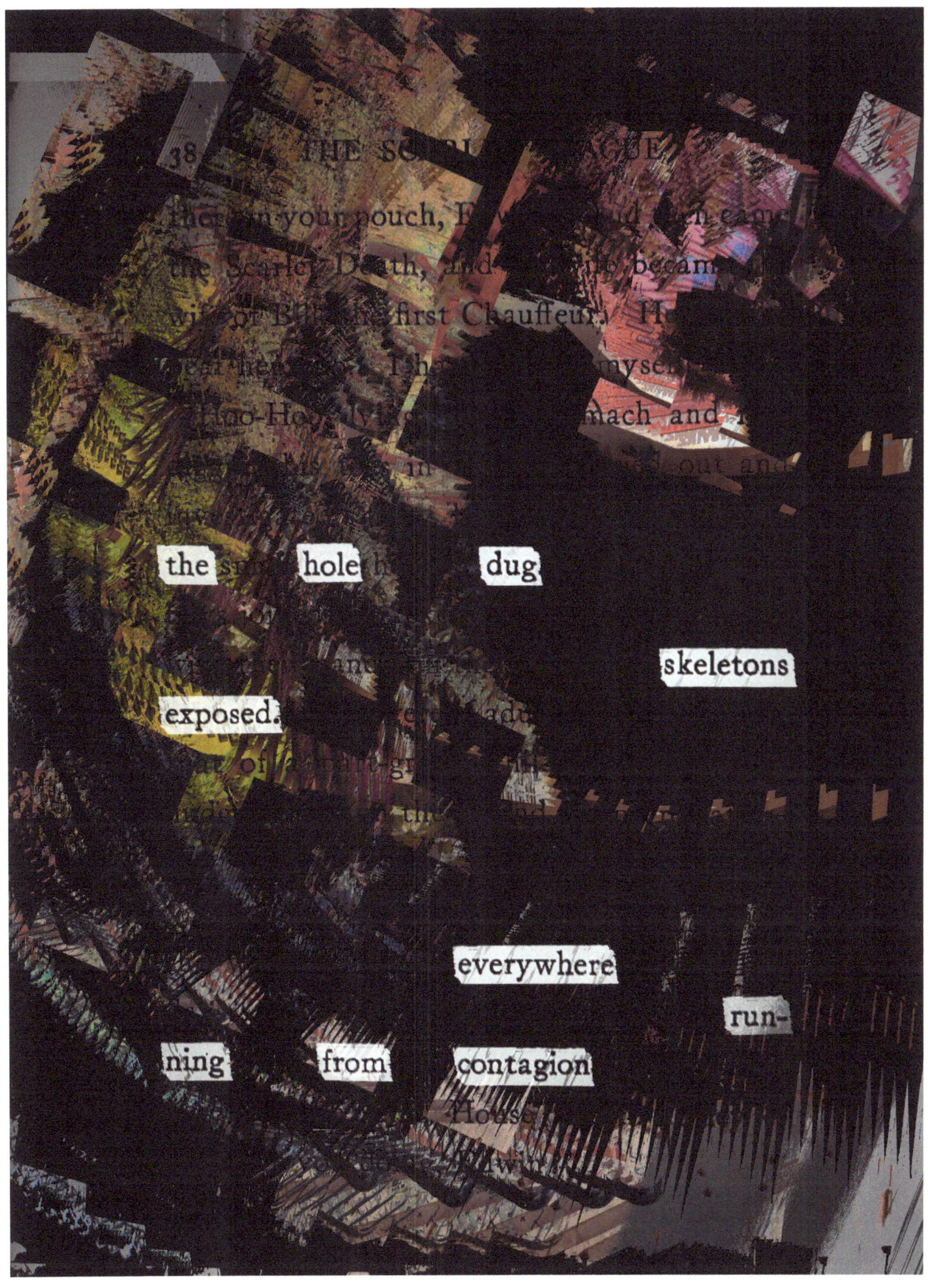

the   hole   dug

skeletons

exposed.

everywhere

run-
ning   from   contagion

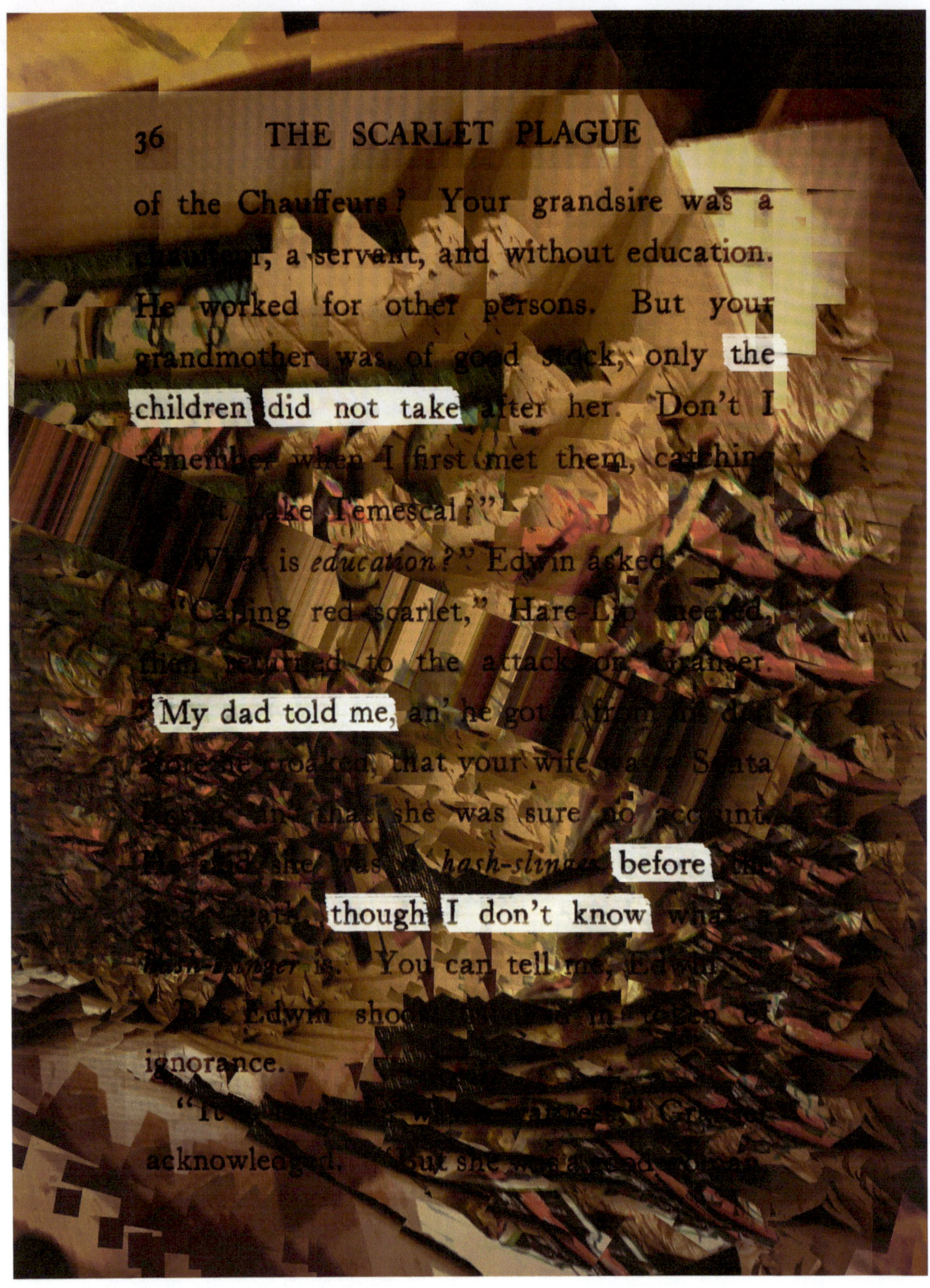

36   THE SCARLET PLAGUE
of the Chauffeurs? Your grandsire was a
chauffeur, a servant, and without education.
He worked for other persons. But your
grandmother was of good stock, only the
children did not take after her. Don't I
remember when I first met them, catching
but at lake Temescal?"
"What is education?" Edwin asked.
"Calling red scarlet," Hare-Lip sneered,
then returned to the attack on Granser.
"My dad told me, an' he got it from his dad
before he croaked, that your wife was a Santa
Rosan, an' that she was sure no account. He
said she was a hash-slinger before the
Death, though I don't know what a
hash-slinger is. You can tell me, Edwin."
But Edwin shook his head in token of
ignorance.
"It is true, she was a waitress," Granser
acknowledged. "But she was a good woman,

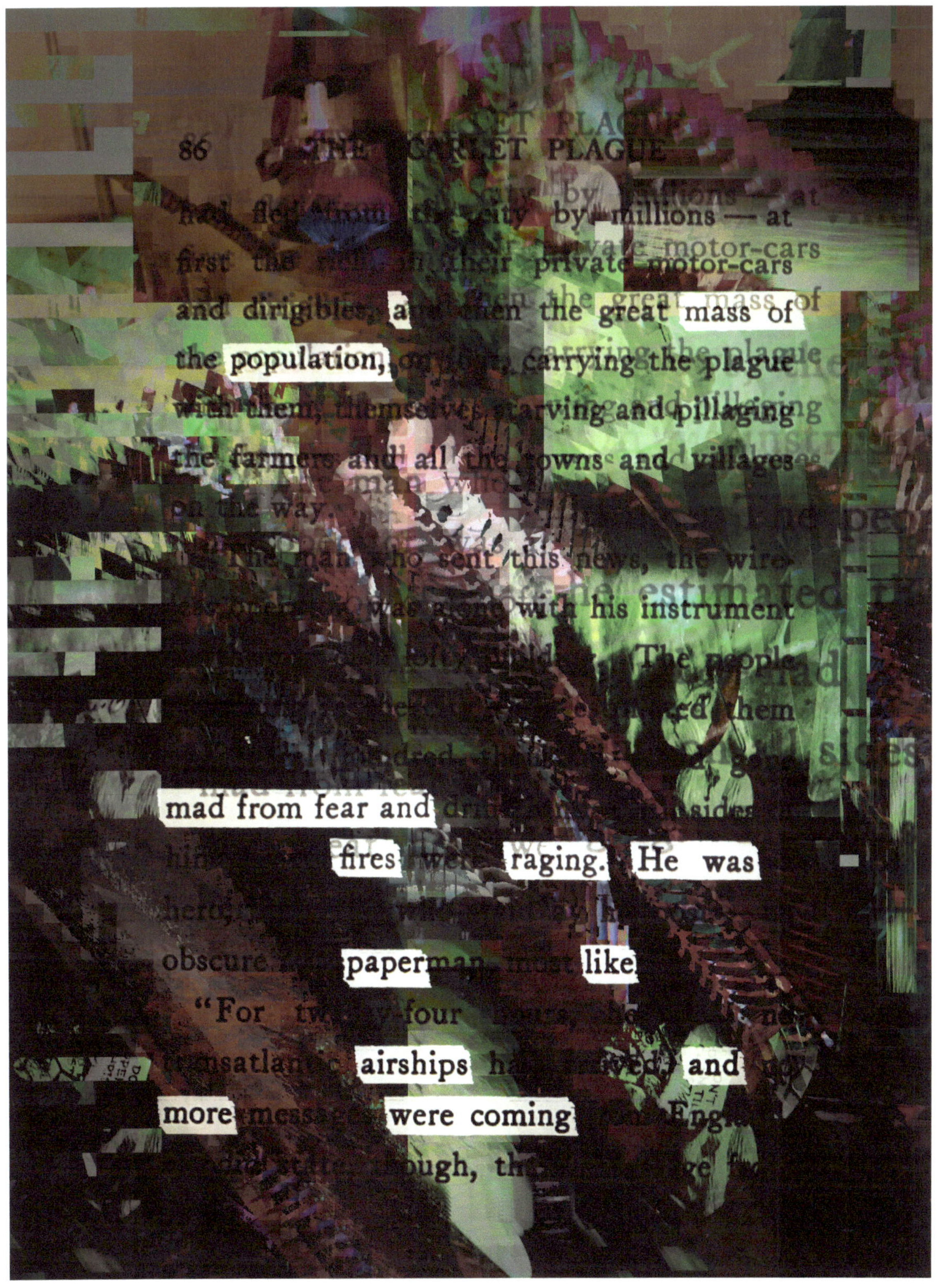
population
mad from fear and
fires were raging. He was
paperman like
airships and
more were coming

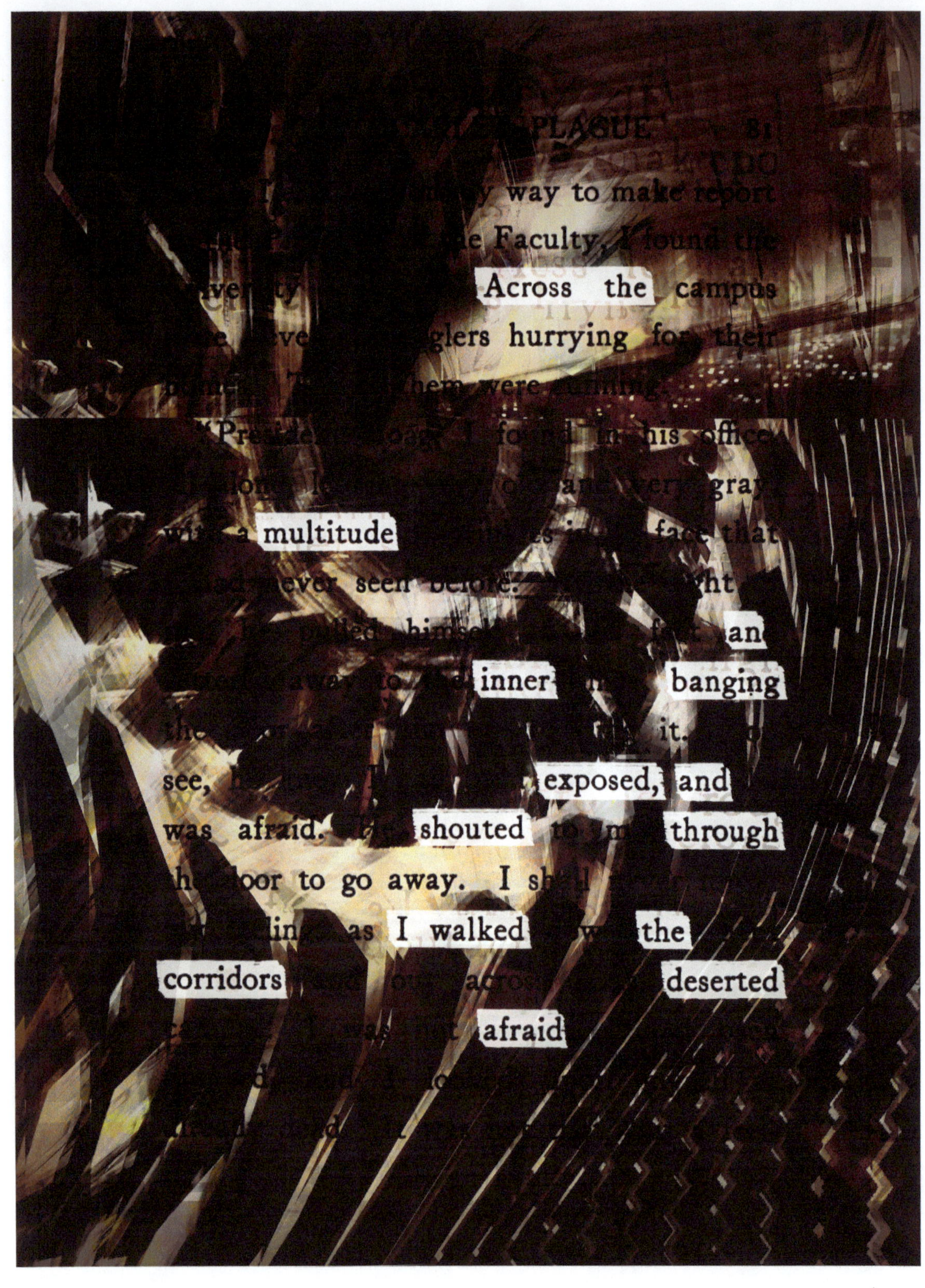
PLAGUE . . . 81
way to make report
Faculty. I found the
Across the campus
glers hurrying for their
hem were running
President . . . I found in his office
are gray
a multitude . . . face that
never seen before
pulled himself . . . feet an
inner . . . banging
it
see . . . exposed, and
was afraid . . . shouted to . . . through
door to go away. I shall
as I walked . . . the
corridors . . . across . . . deserted
afraid

BOOKSHELF WITH DANTE & WAX SEAL

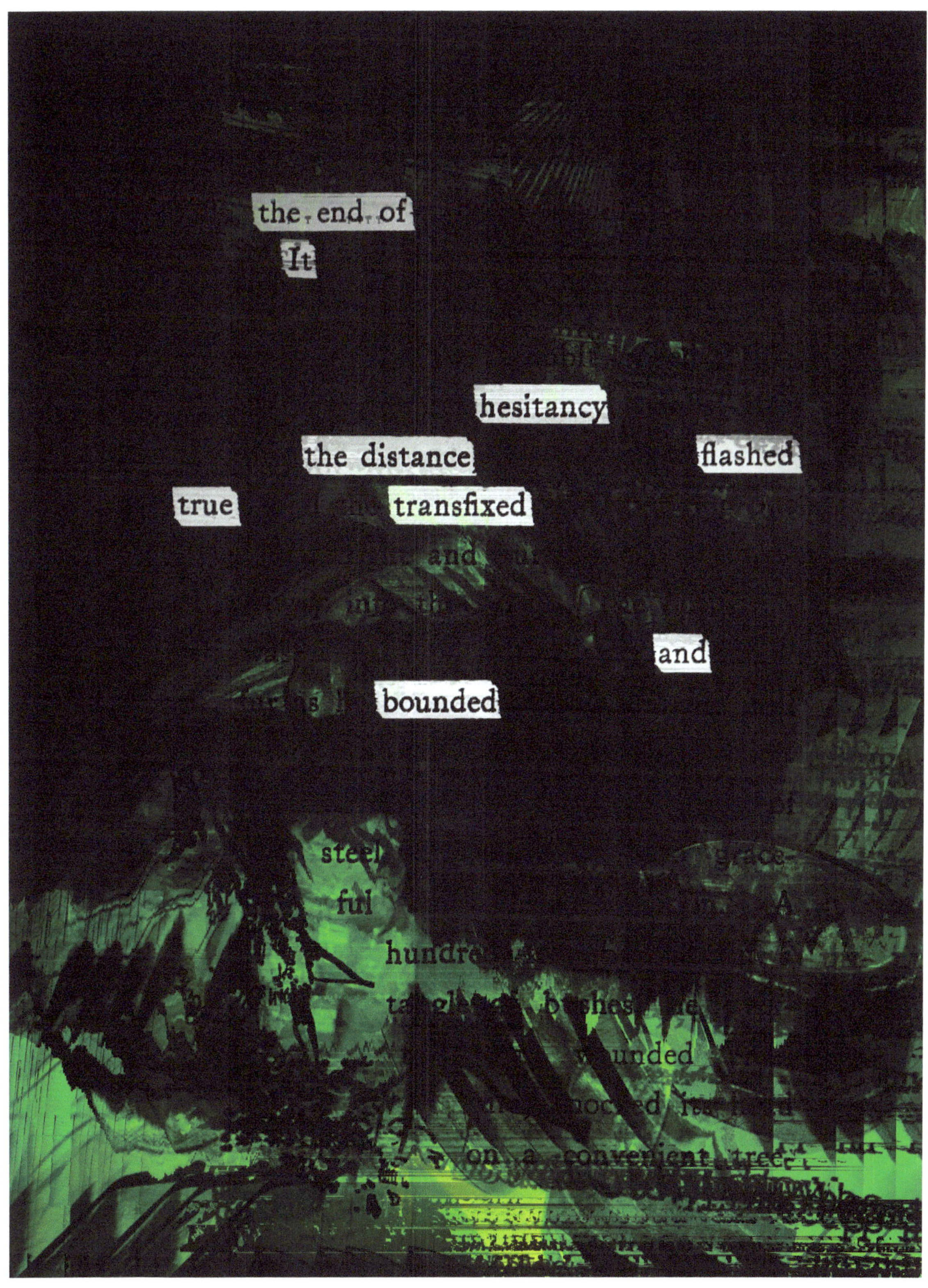

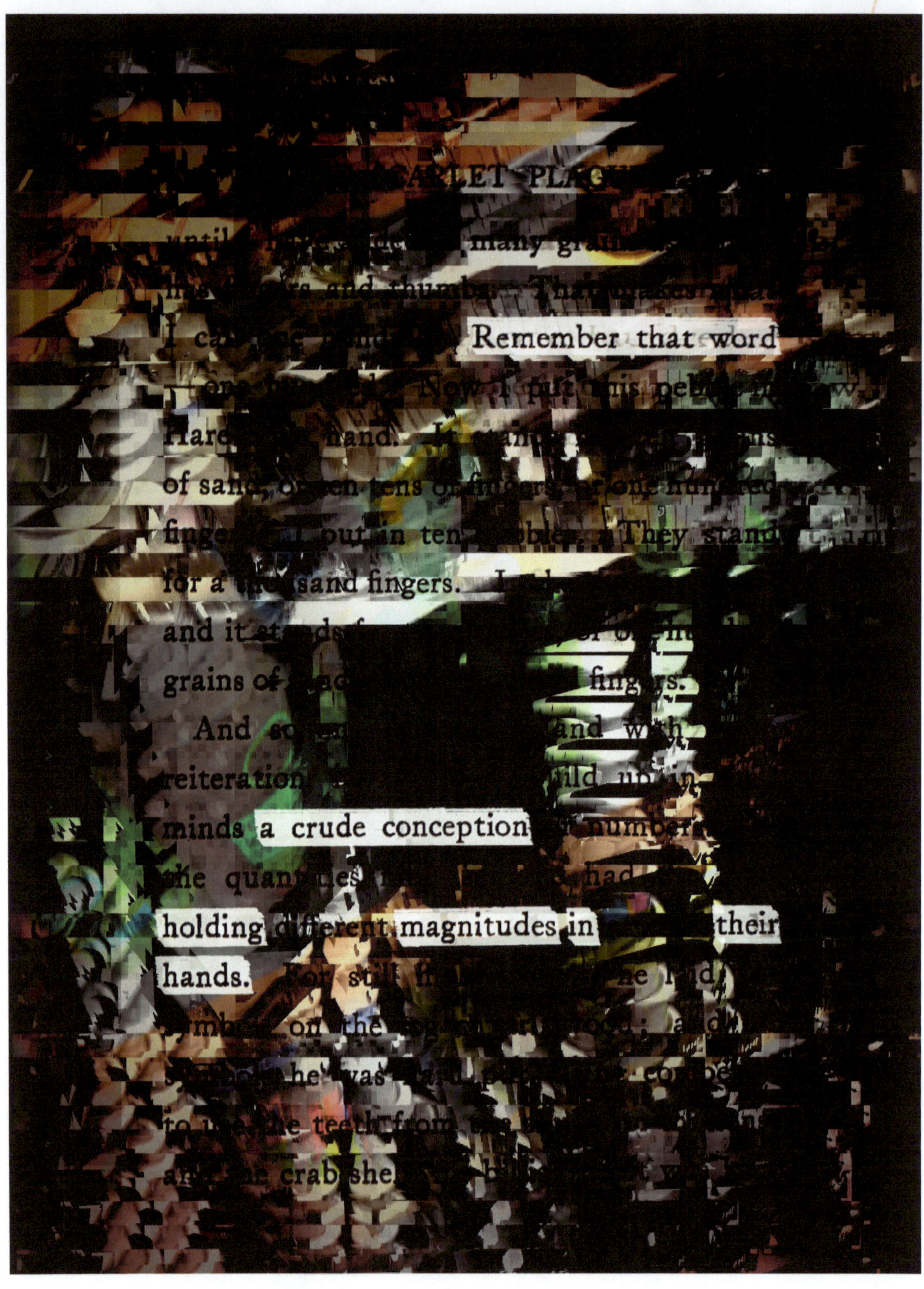
Remember that word
minds a crude conception
holding different magnitudes in   their
hands.

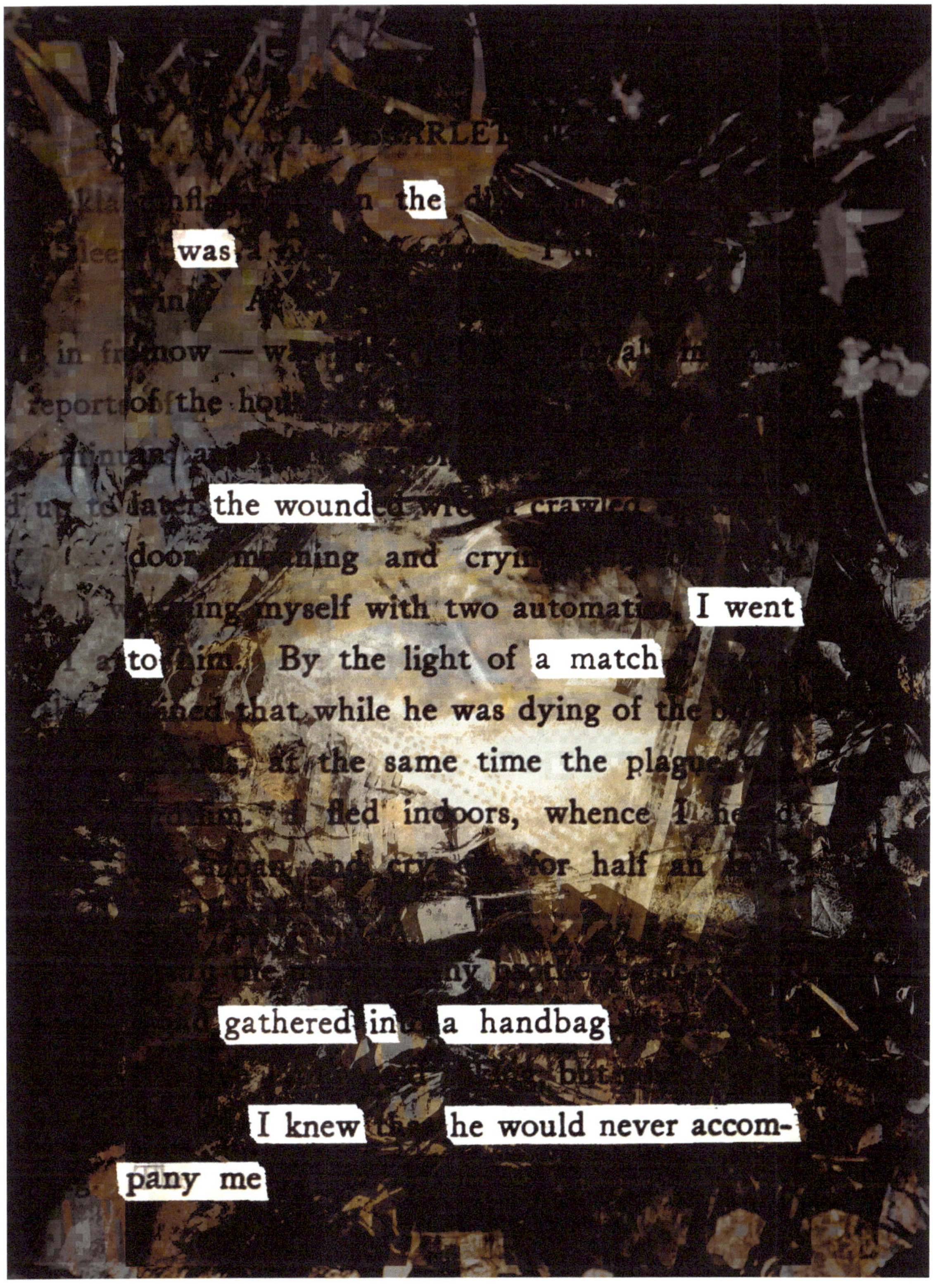
the
was
the wounded
I went
a match
gathered in a handbag
I knew   he would never accom-
pany me

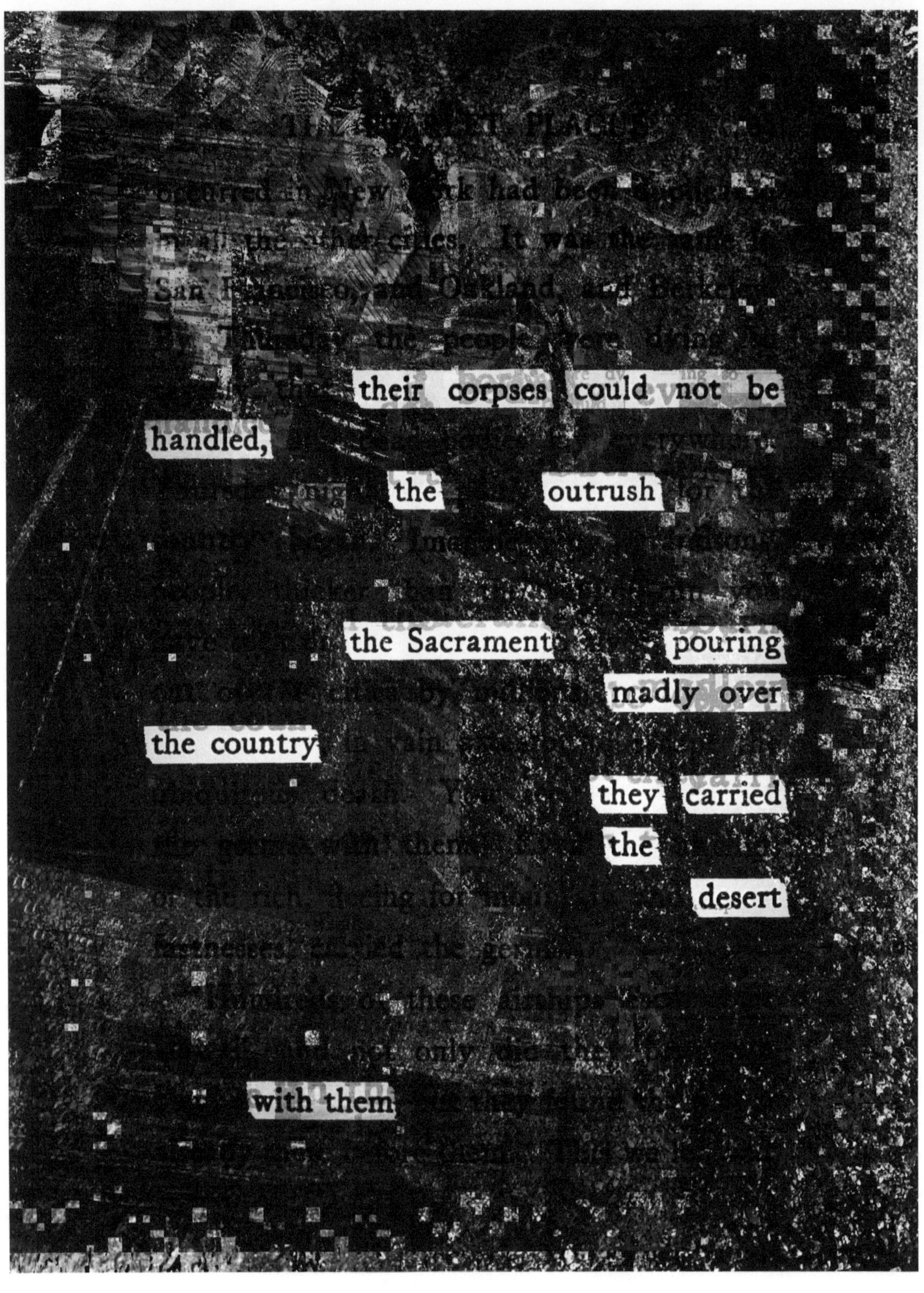

their corpses could not be
handled,
the outrush
the Sacramento pouring
madly over
the country
they carried
the
desert
with them

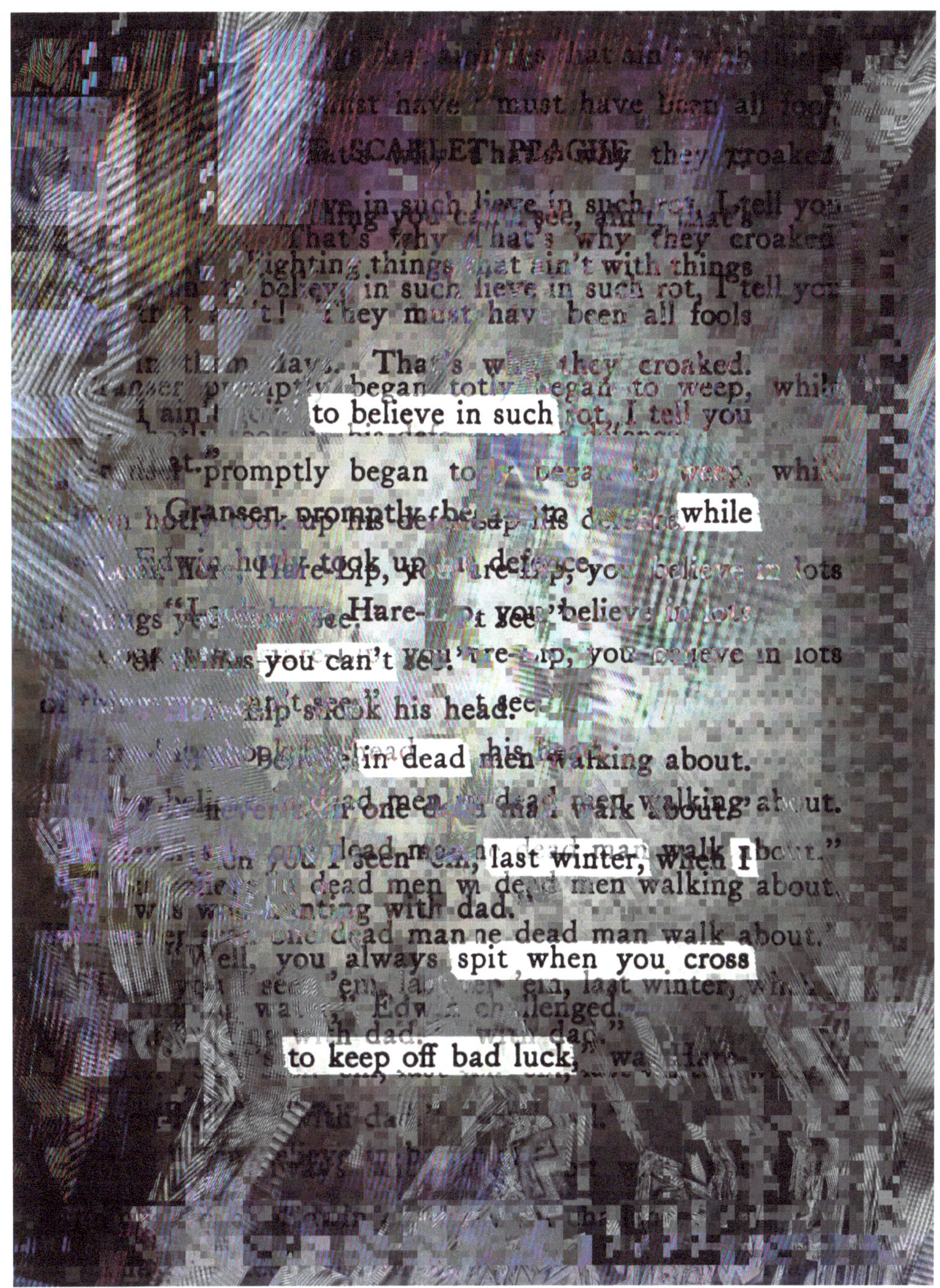
to believe in such rot, I tell you
while
you can't you're up, you believe in lots
in dead men walking about.
last winter, when I
spit when you cross
to keep off bad luck,

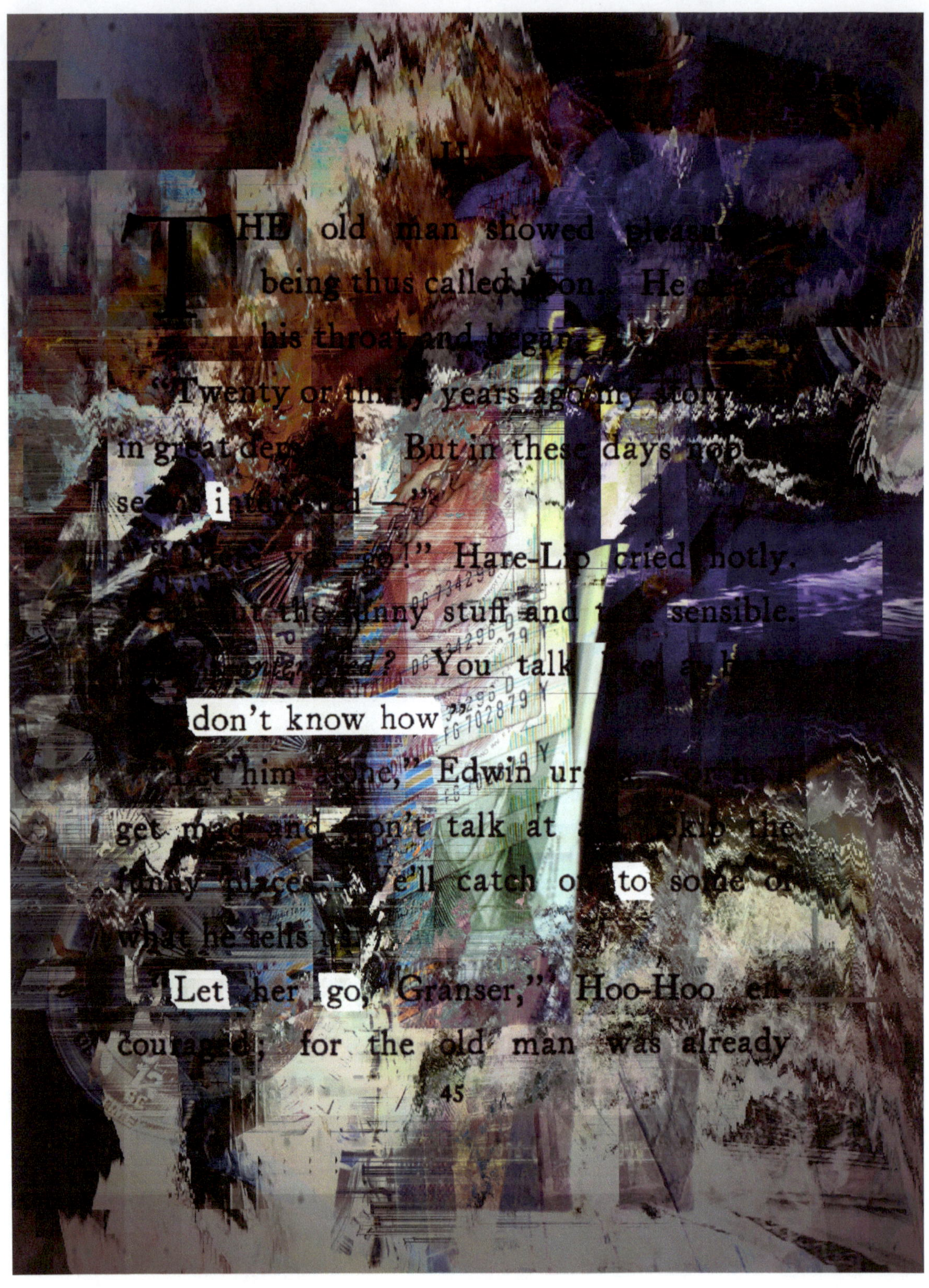

II

THE old man showed pleasure
being thus called upon. He cleared
his throat and began.
"Twenty or thirty years ago my story
in great demand. But in these days nob
seems interested—"
"There you go!" Hare-Lip cried hotly.
Cut out the funny stuff and talk sensible.
Interested? You talk like a
don't know how."
"Let him alone," Edwin urged.
get mad and won't talk at all. Skip the
funny places. We'll catch on to some of
what he tells us.
"Let her go, Granser," Hoo-Hoo en
couraged; for the old man was already

45

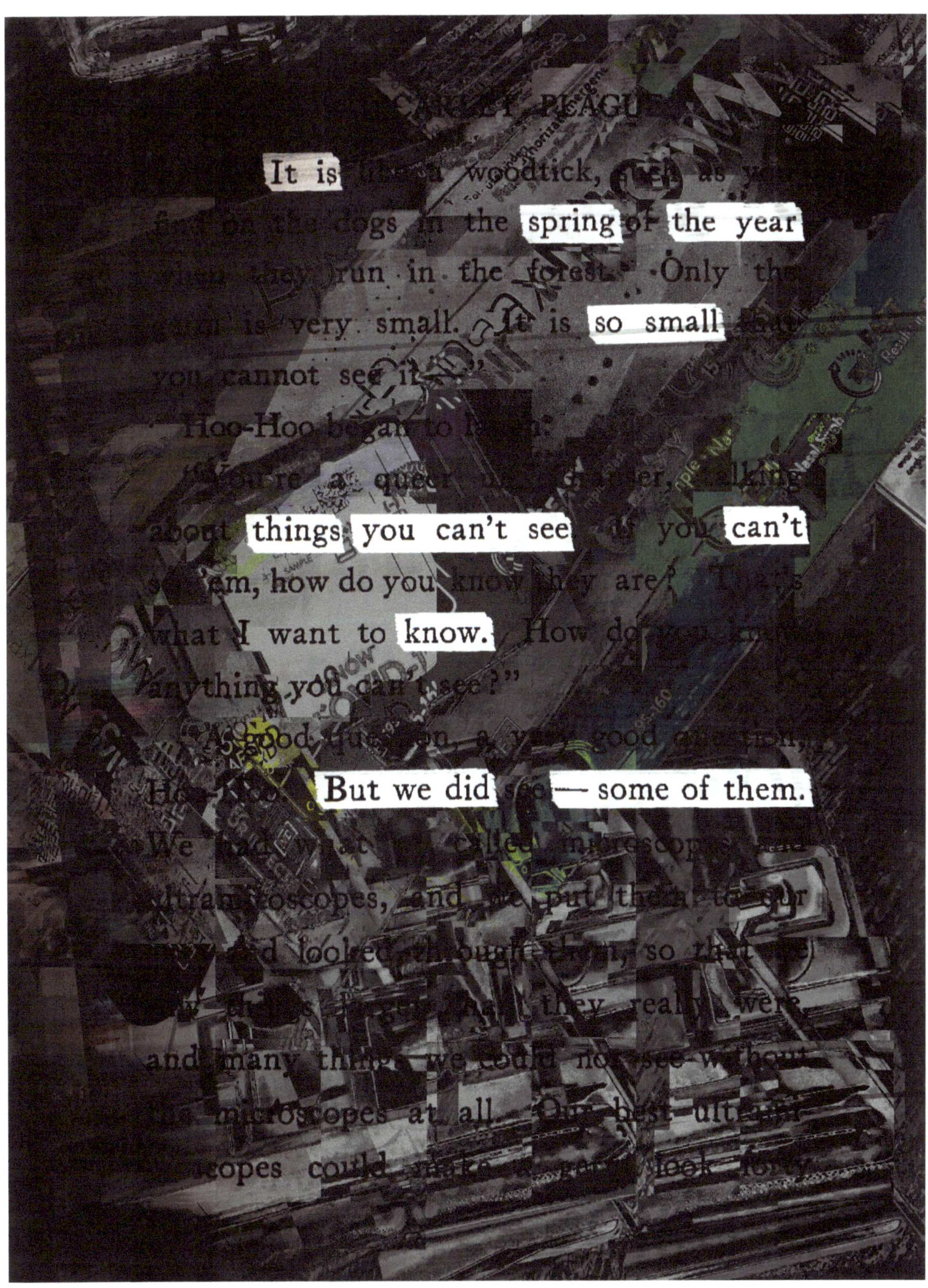
SCARLET PLAGUE
It is like a woodtick, such as you
find on the dogs in the spring of the year
when they run in the forest. Only this
germ is very small. It is so small that
you cannot see it—"
Hoo-Hoo began to laugh.
"You're a queer bear-chaser, talking
about things you can't see. If you can't
see 'em, how do you know they are? That's
what I want to know. How do you know
anything you can't see?"
"A good question, a very good question,
Hoo-Hoo. But we did see—some of them.
We had what we called microscopes and
ultramicroscopes, and we put them to our
eyes and looked through them, so that we
could see things far larger than they really were,
and many things we could not see without
the microscopes at all. Our best ultra-
scopes could make a germ look forty

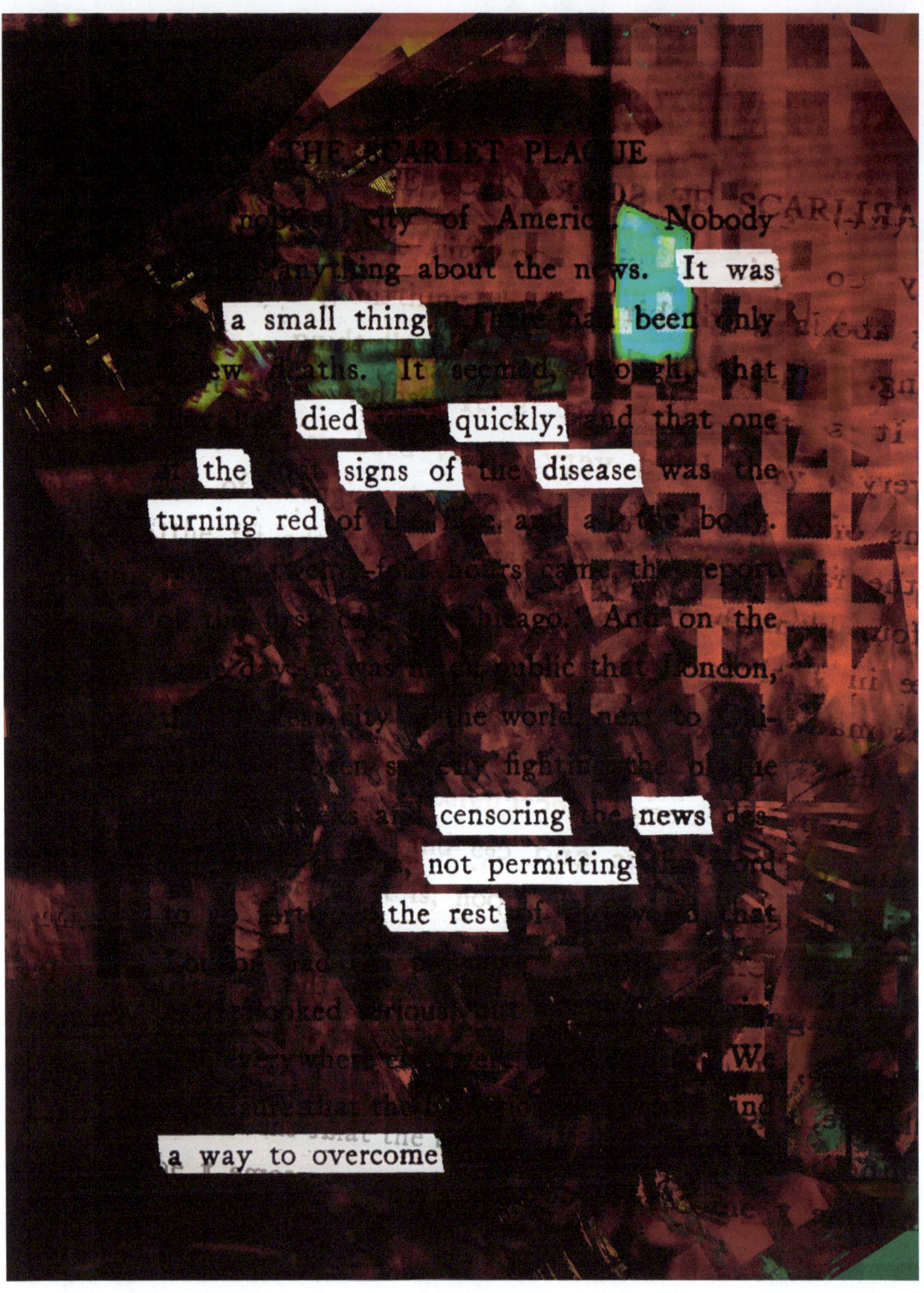
a small thing
died quickly,
signs of the disease was the
turning red
censoring the news
not permitting
the rest
a way to overcome

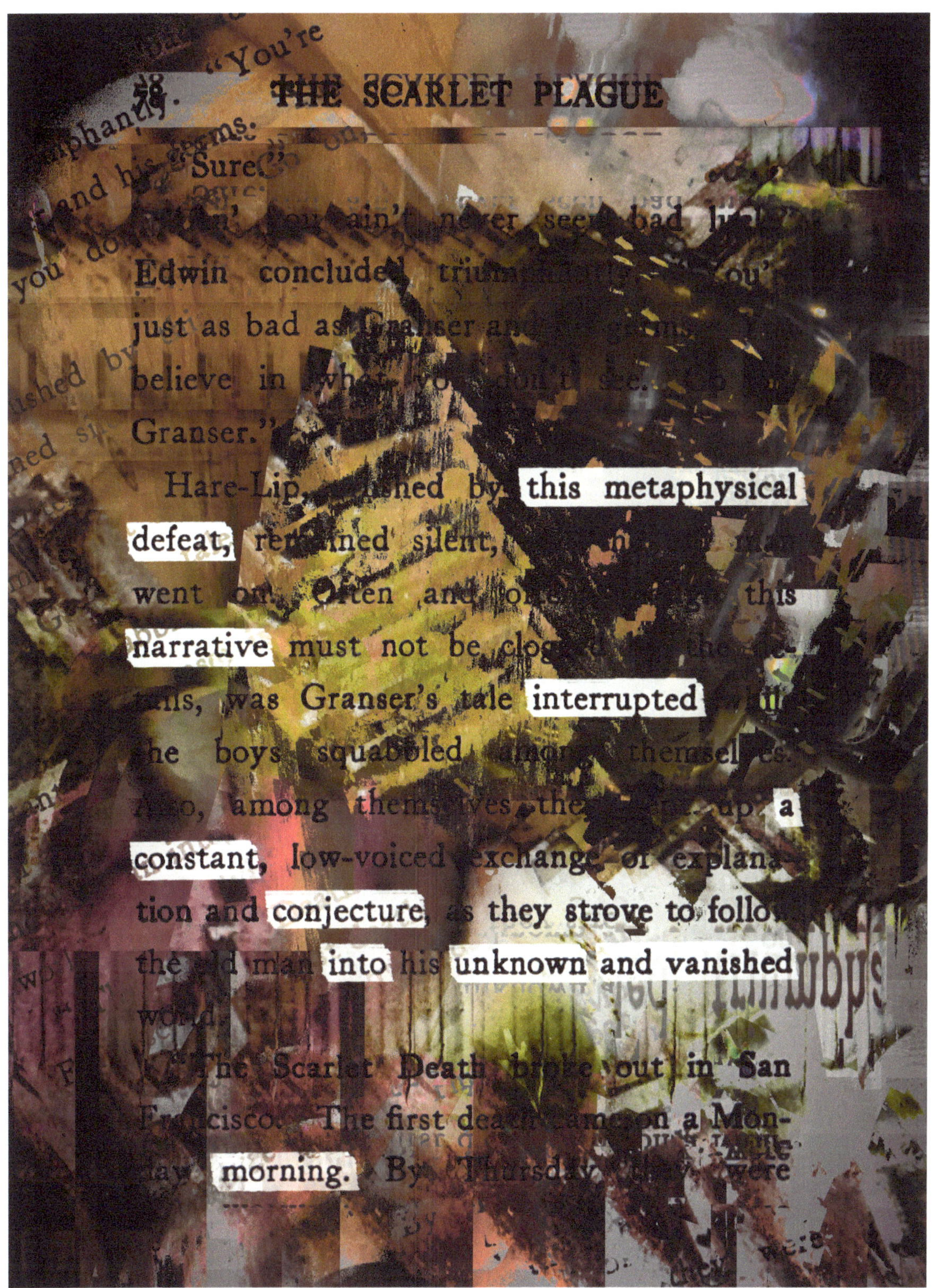
58. THE SCARLET PLAGUE
"You're
and his germs:
"Sure."
you don't
you ain't never seen bad luck,"
Edwin concluded triumphantly. "You're
just as bad as Granser and his germs. You
believe in what you don't see. Look at
Granser."
Hare-Lip, crushed by this metaphysical
defeat, remained silent, ...
went on. Often and oftener ... this
narrative must not be clogged ... the de-
tails, was Granser's tale interrupted. ...
the boys squabbled among themselves.
Also, among themselves they kept up a
constant, low-voiced exchange of explana-
tion and conjecture, as they strove to follow
the old man into his unknown and vanished
world.
"The Scarlet Death broke out in San
Francisco. The first death came on a Mon-
day morning. By Thursday they were

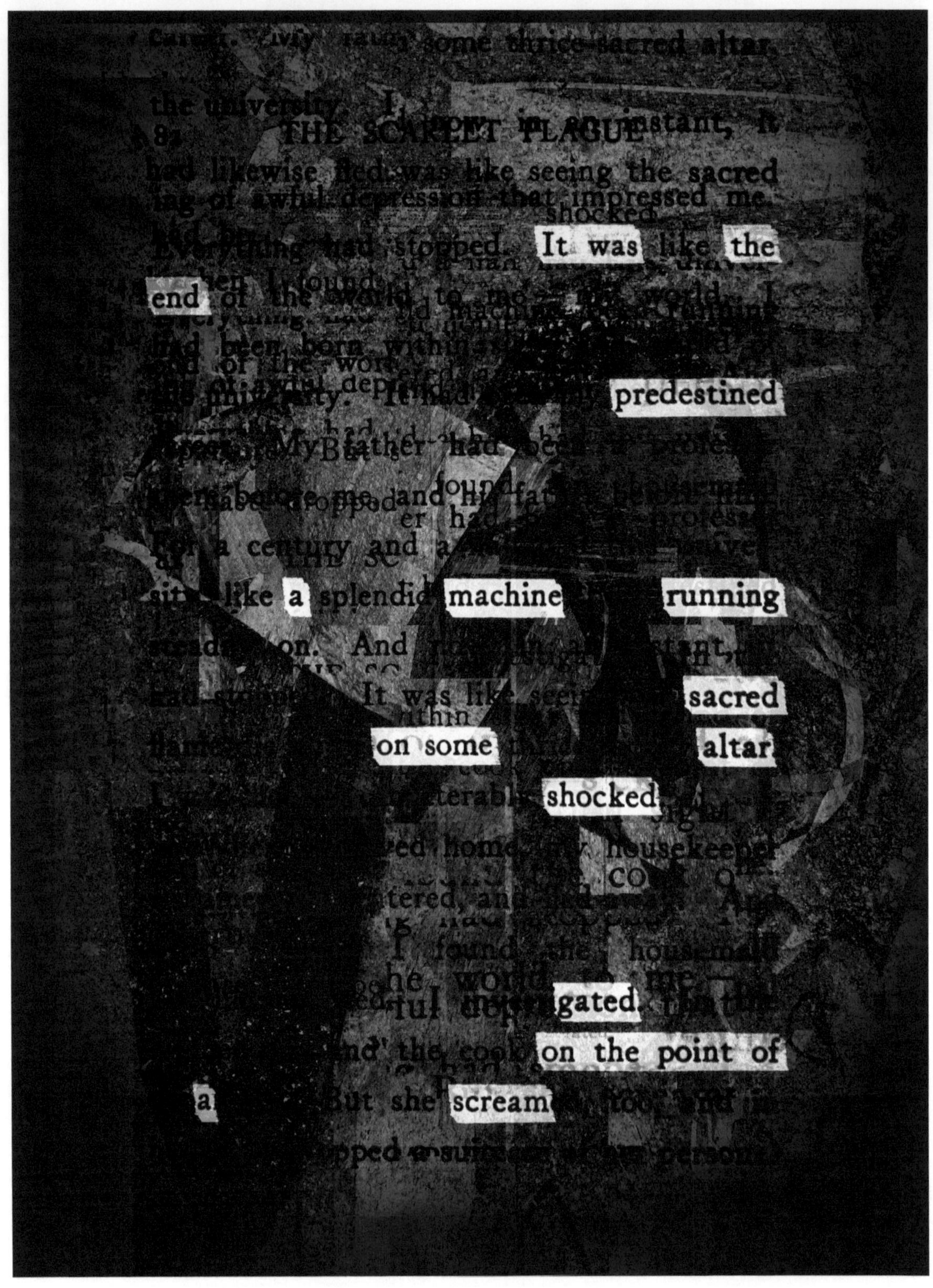
It was like the
end of the world to me — my world. I
predestined
machine   running
sacred
on some   altar
shocked
on the point of

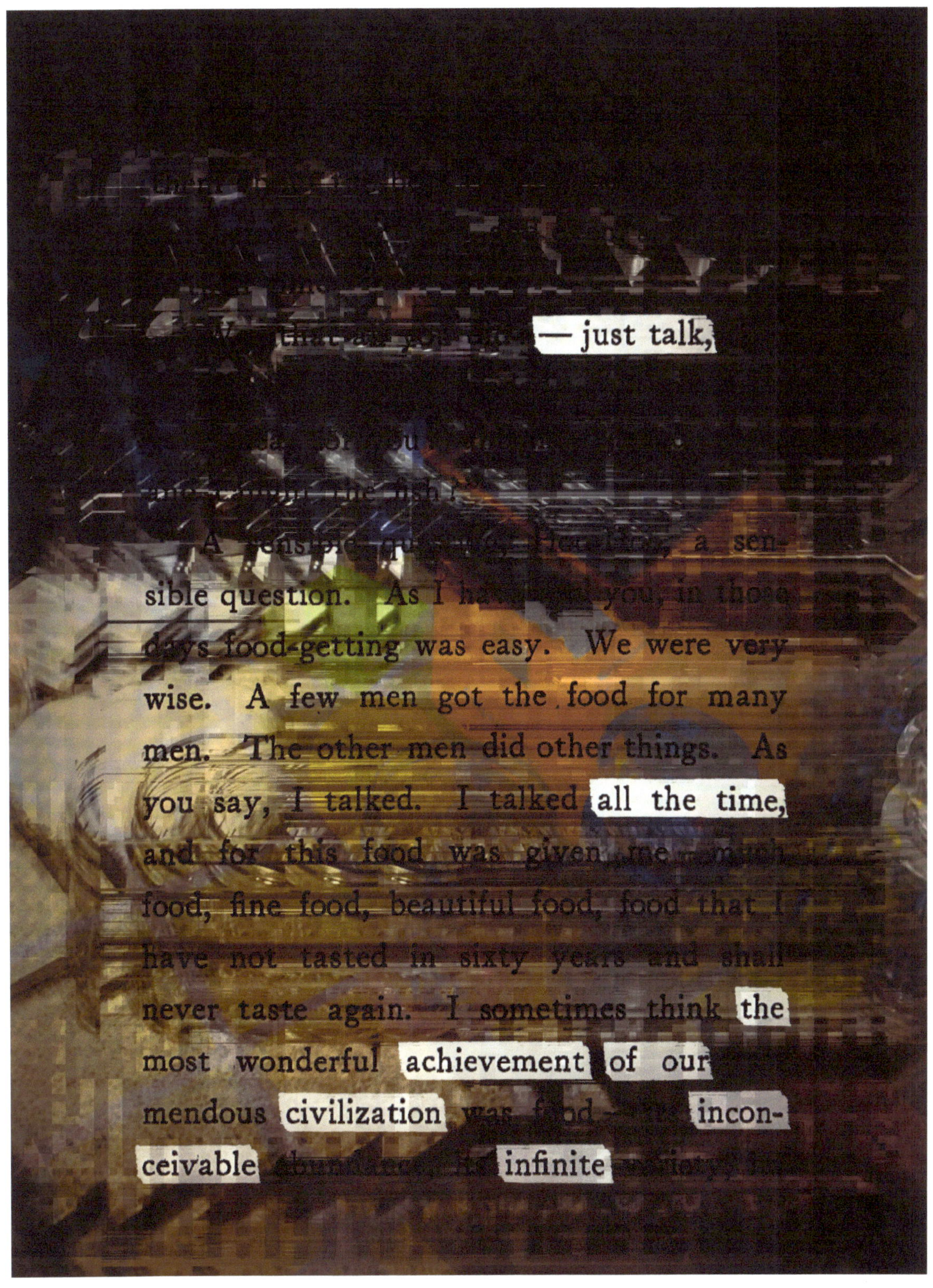
— just talk,

A sensible question, Heretira, a sensible question. As I have told you, in those days food-getting was easy. We were very wise. A few men got the food for many men. The other men did other things. As you say, I talked. I talked all the time, and for this food was given me — much food, fine food, beautiful food, food that I have not tasted in sixty years and shall never taste again. I sometimes think the most wonderful achievement of our mendous civilization was food — its inconceivable abundance, its infinite variety,

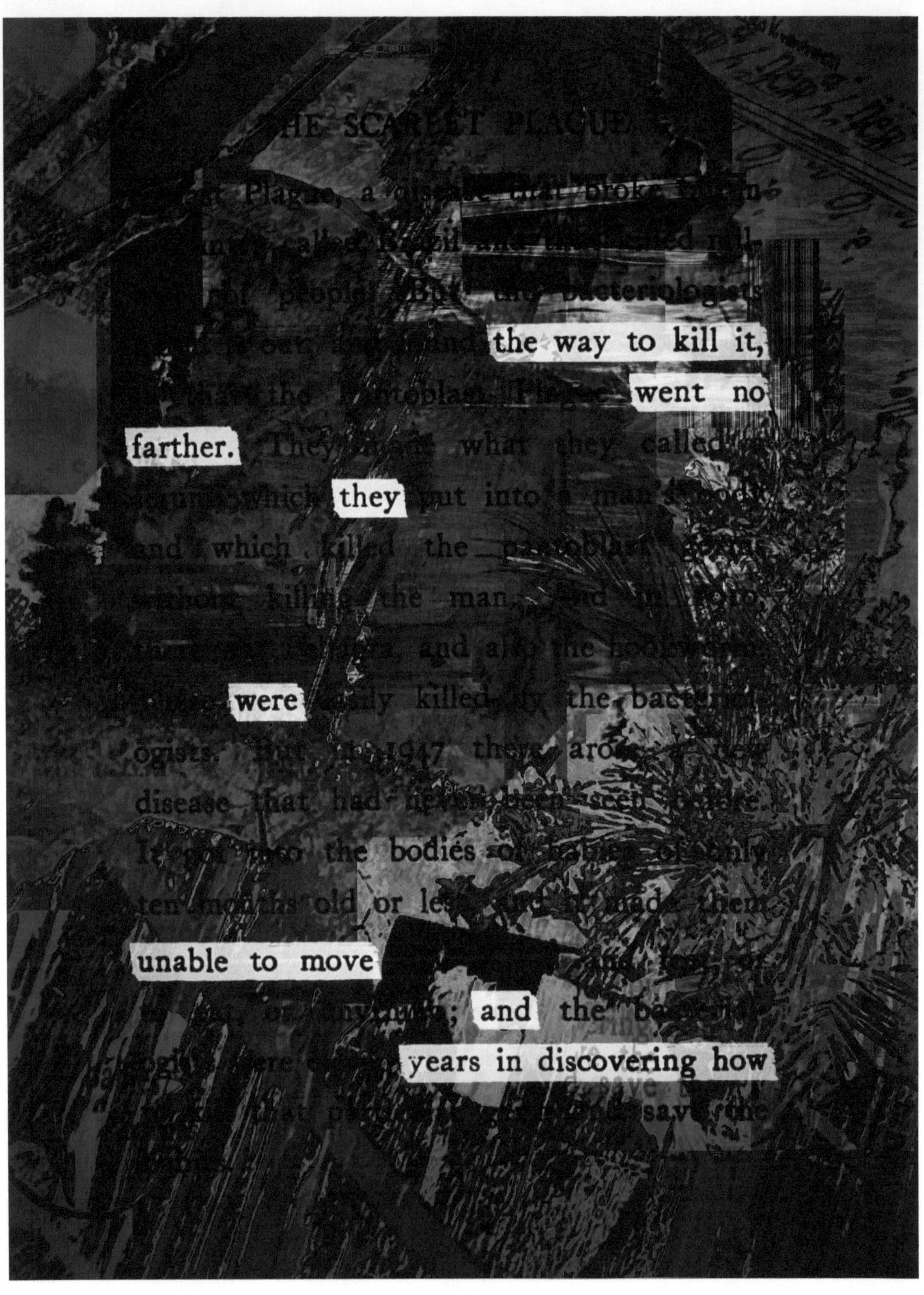
the way to kill it,
went no
farther.
they
were
unable to move
and
years in discovering how

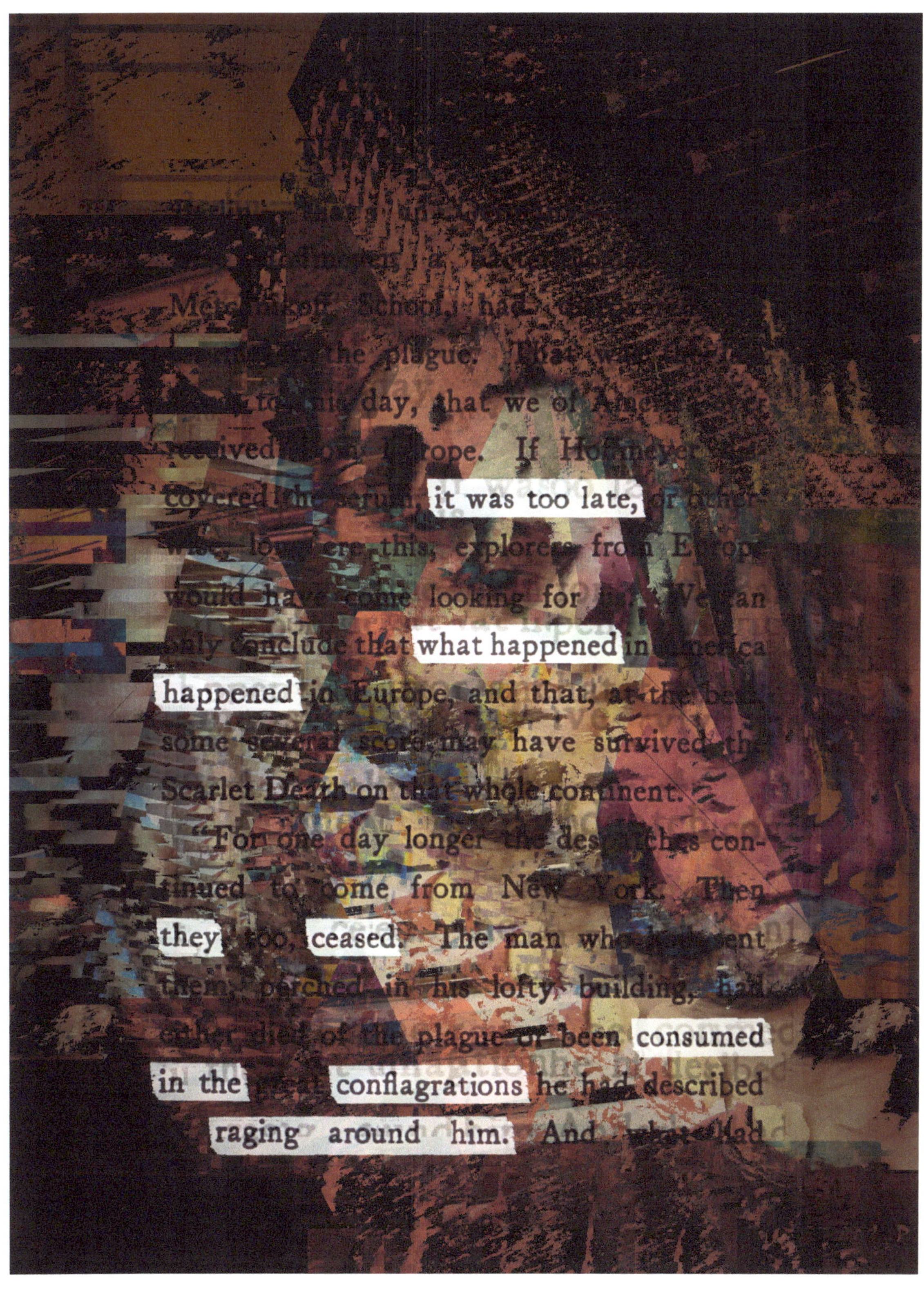

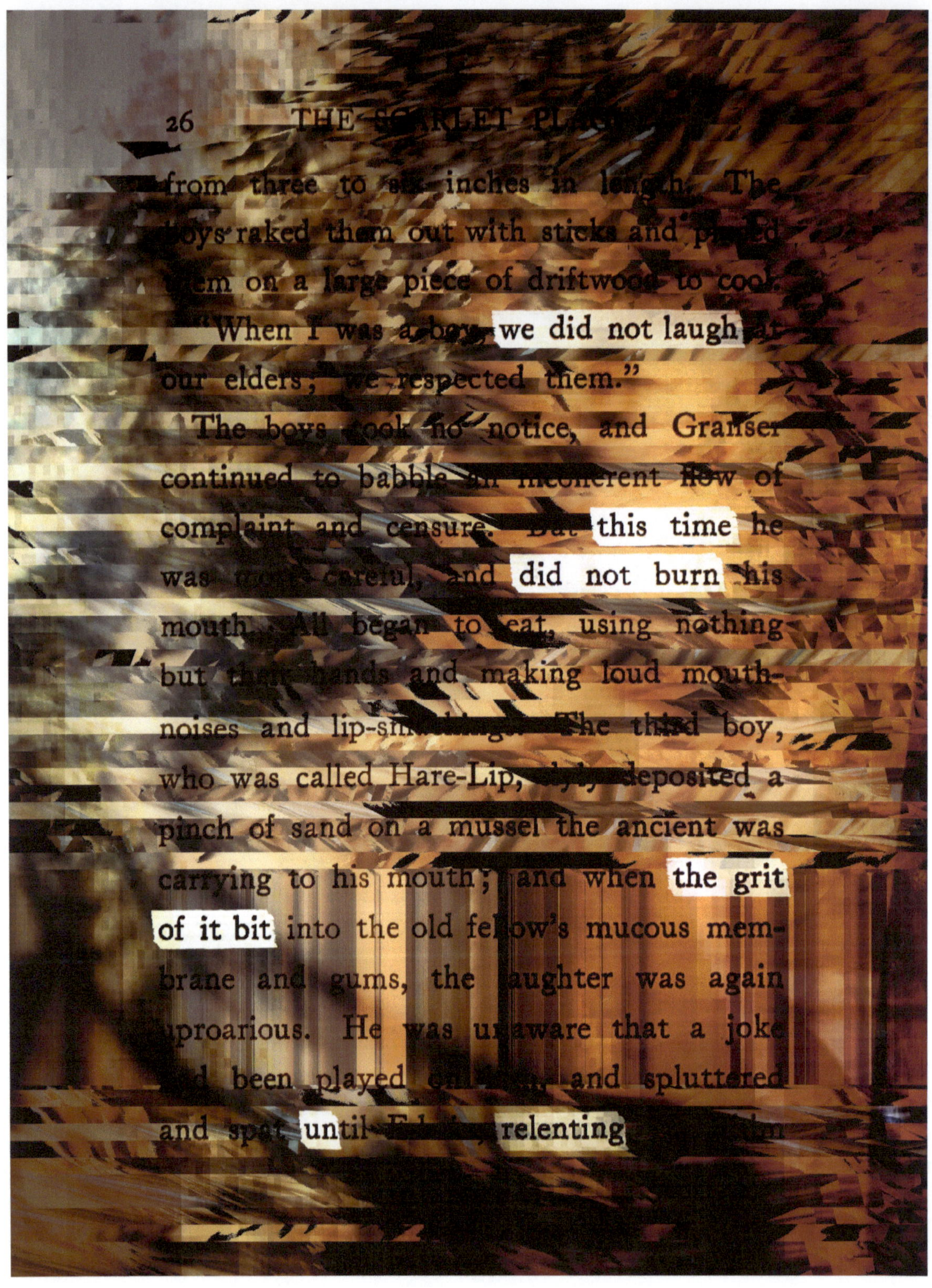

26 THE SCARLET PLAGUE

from three to six inches in length. The boys raked them out with sticks and placed them on a large piece of driftwood to cool.

"When I was a boy, we did not laugh at our elders; we respected them."

The boys took no notice, and Granser continued to babble an incoherent flow of complaint and censure. But this time he was more careful, and did not burn his mouth. All began to eat, using nothing but their hands and making loud mouth-noises and lip-smackings. The third boy, who was called Hare-Lip, slyly deposited a pinch of sand on a mussel the ancient was carrying to his mouth; and when the grit of it bit into the old fellow's mucous membrane and gums, the laughter was again uproarious. He was unaware that a joke had been played on him, and spluttered and spat until Edwin, relenting, gave him

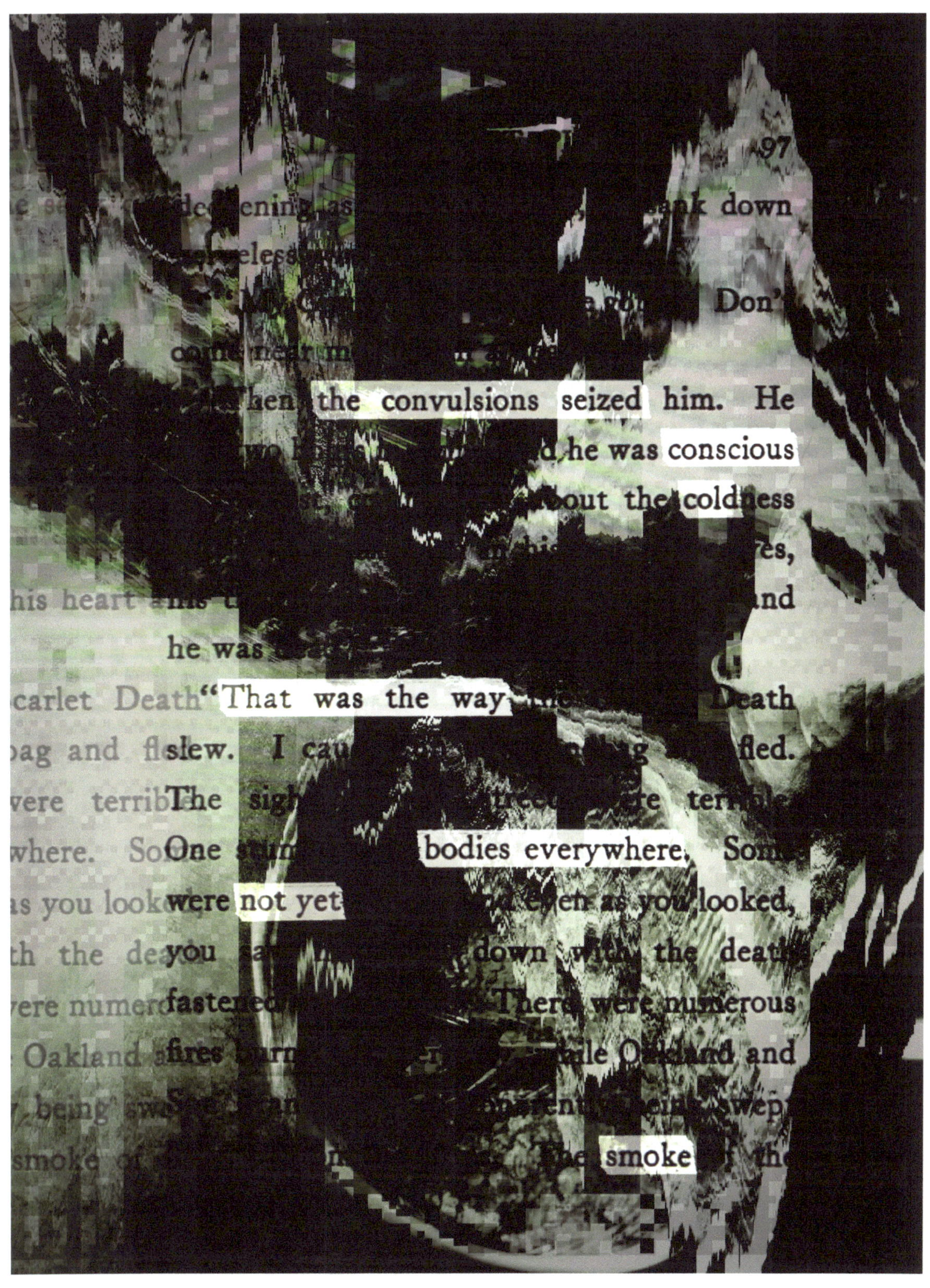
97
e se deadening as sank down
voiceless
Don'
come near
hen the convulsions seized him. He
he was conscious
out the coldness
es,
his heart and
he was
carlet Death "That was the way Death
bag and fl slew. I cau fled.
were terrib The sigh ted were terrible
where. So One bodies everywhere. Som
as you look were not yet even as you looked,
th the dea you down with the death
were numer fastened There were numerous
Oakland fires burn tile Oakland and
being swe apparently being swep
smoke of The smoke of the

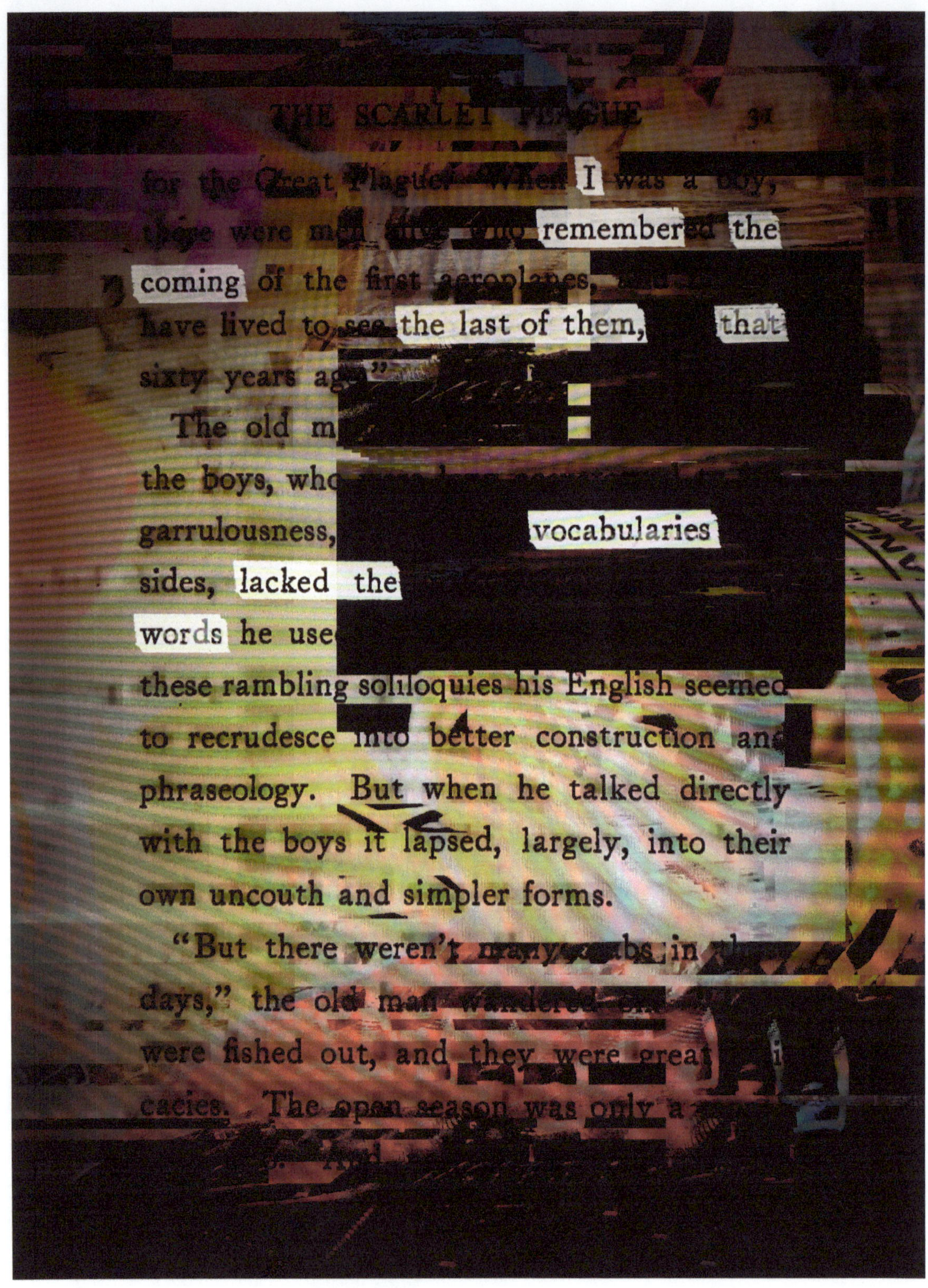
THE SCARLET PLAGUE
for the Great Plague. When I was a boy,
there were men alive who remembered the
coming of the first aeroplanes,
have lived to see the last of them, that
sixty years ago."
The old m
the boys, who
garrulousness, vocabularies
sides, lacked the
words he use
these rambling soliloquies his English seemed
to recrudesce into better construction and
phraseology. But when he talked directly
with the boys it lapsed, largely, into their
own uncouth and simpler forms.
"But there weren't many
days," the old man wandered
were fished out, and they were great
cacies. The open season was only a

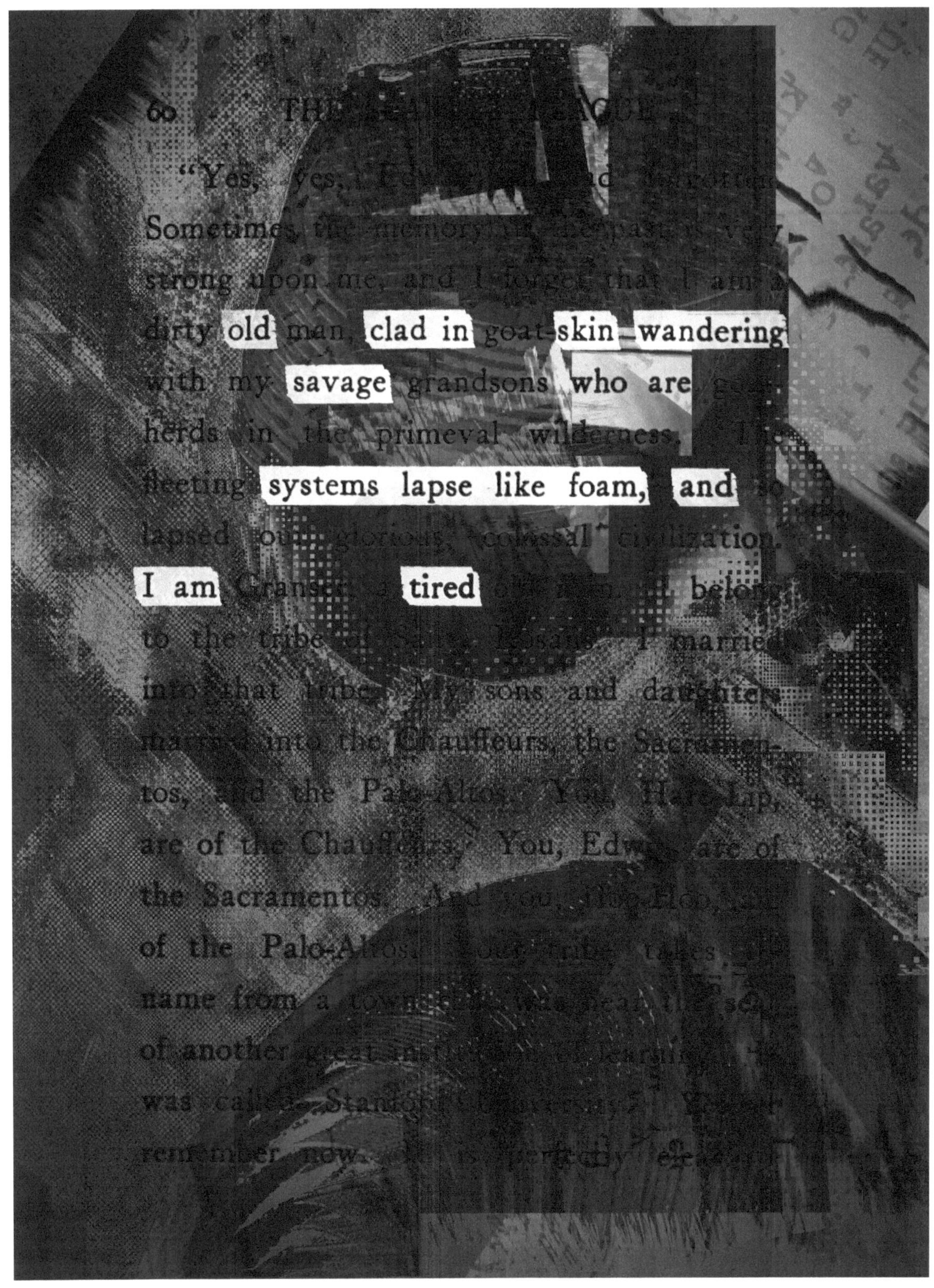
old
clad in goat-skin wandering
savage who are
systems lapse like foam, and
I am tired

Caffè Macchiato, Cloth Napkin

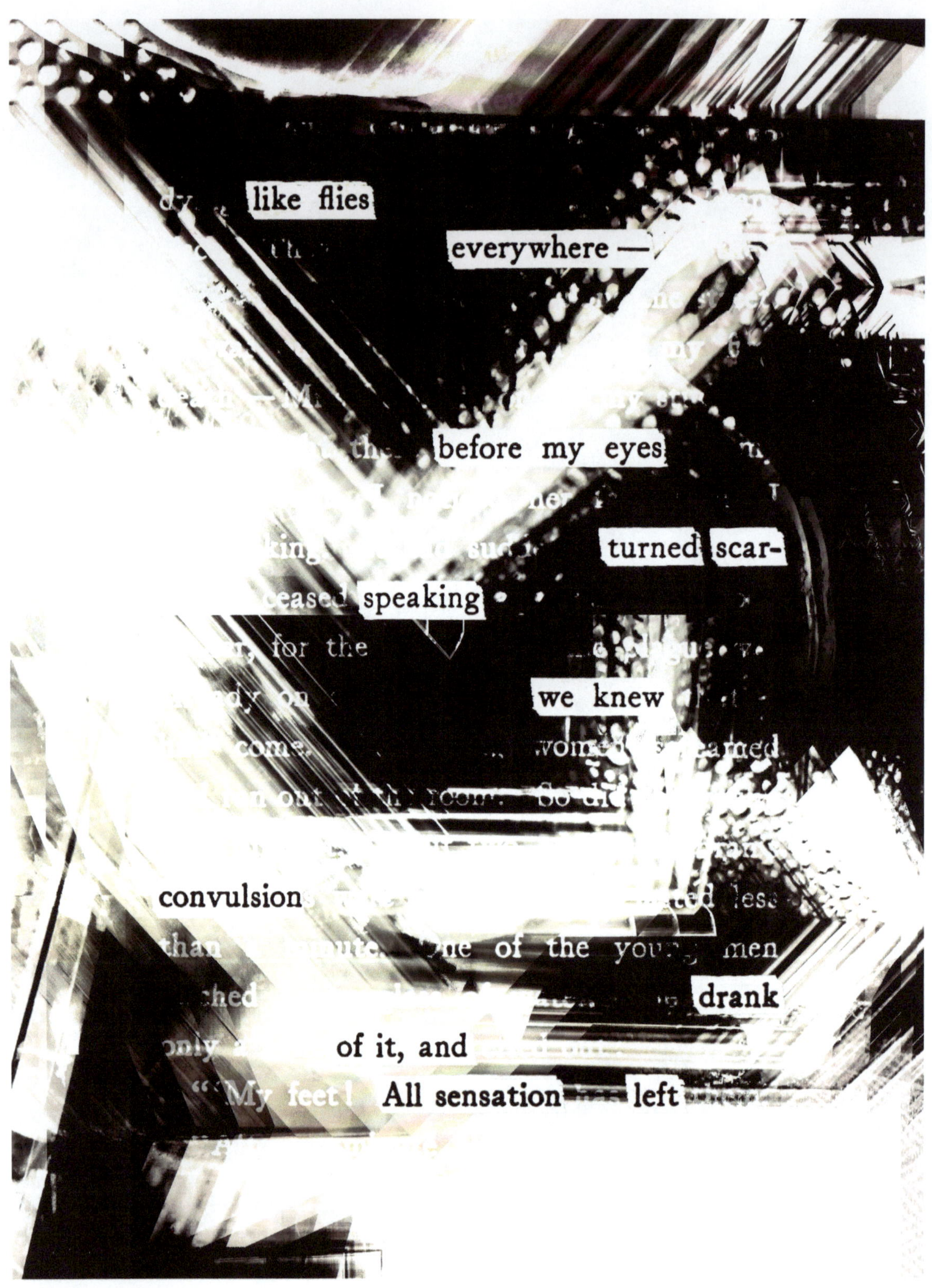

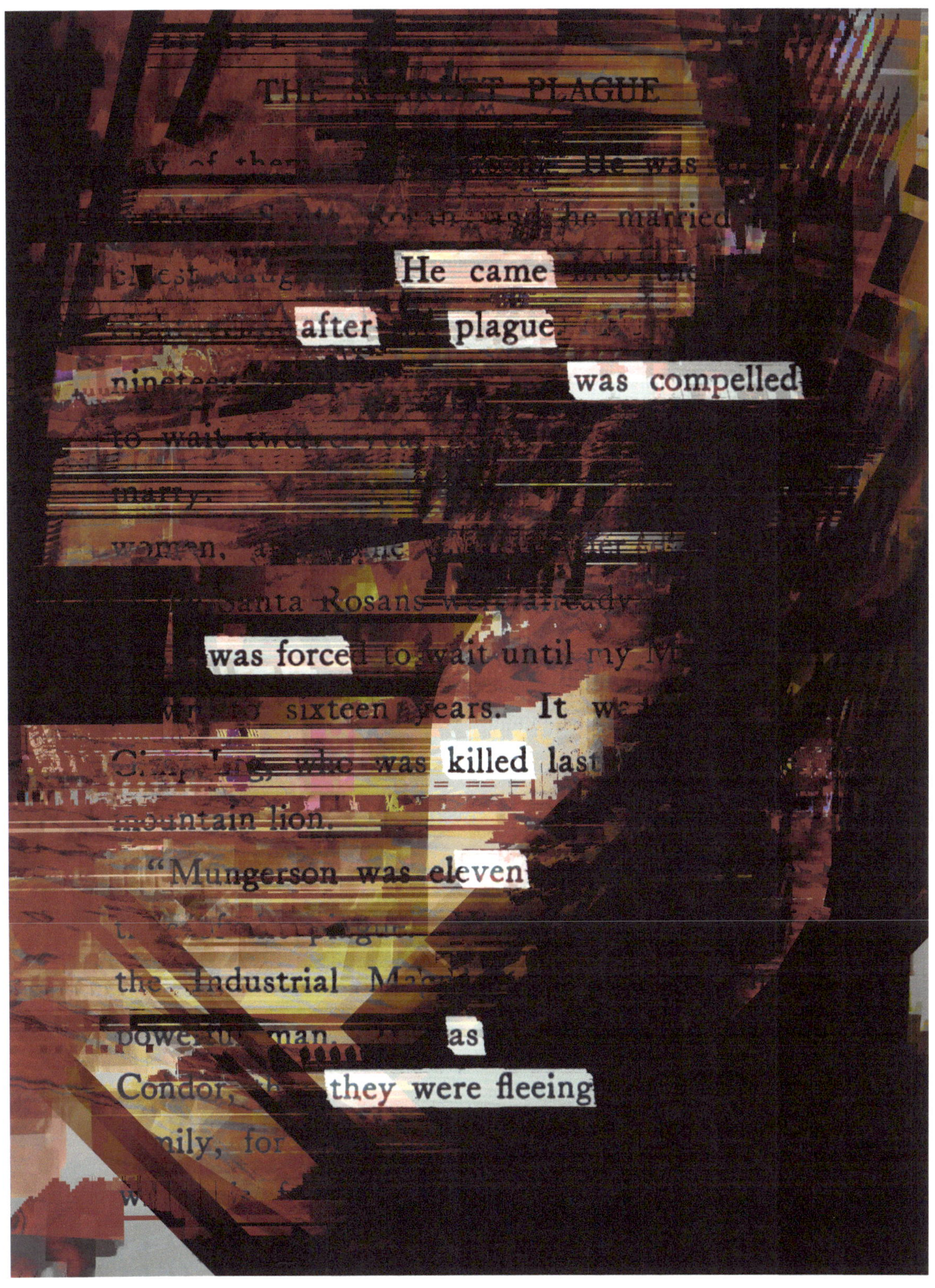
THE SCARLET PLAGUE
He came
after plague
was compelled
was forced to wait until my
killed last
"Mungerson was eleven
as
they were fleeing

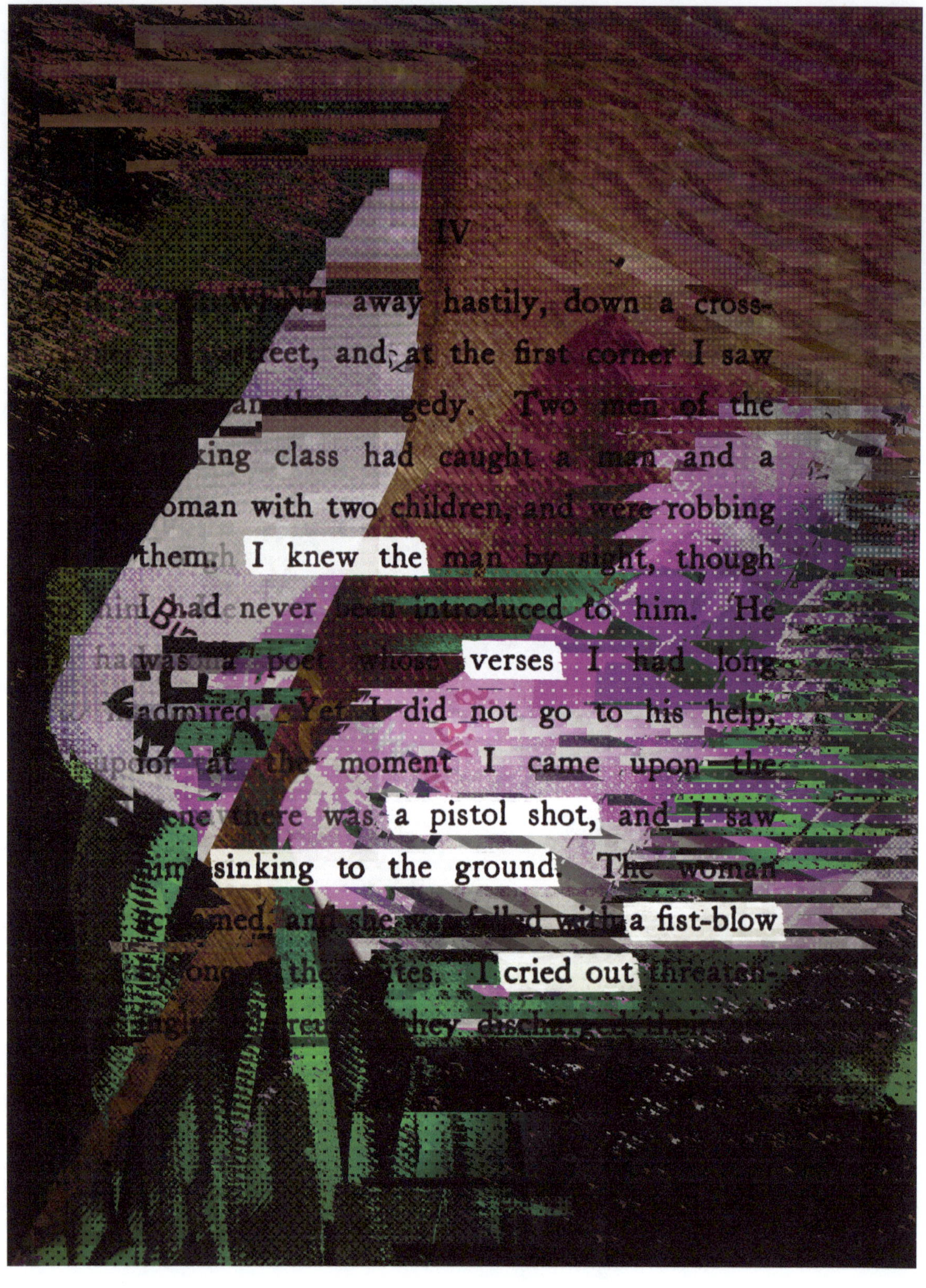
IV

I WENT away hastily, down a cross-
street, and at the first corner I saw
another tragedy. Two men of the
working class had caught a man and a
woman with two children, and were robbing
them. I knew the man by sight, though
I had never been introduced to him. He
was a poet whose verses I had long
admired. Yet I did not go to his help,
for at the moment I came upon the
scene there was a pistol shot, and I saw
him sinking to the ground. The woman
screamed, and she was felled with a fist-blow
among the brutes. I cried out threaten-

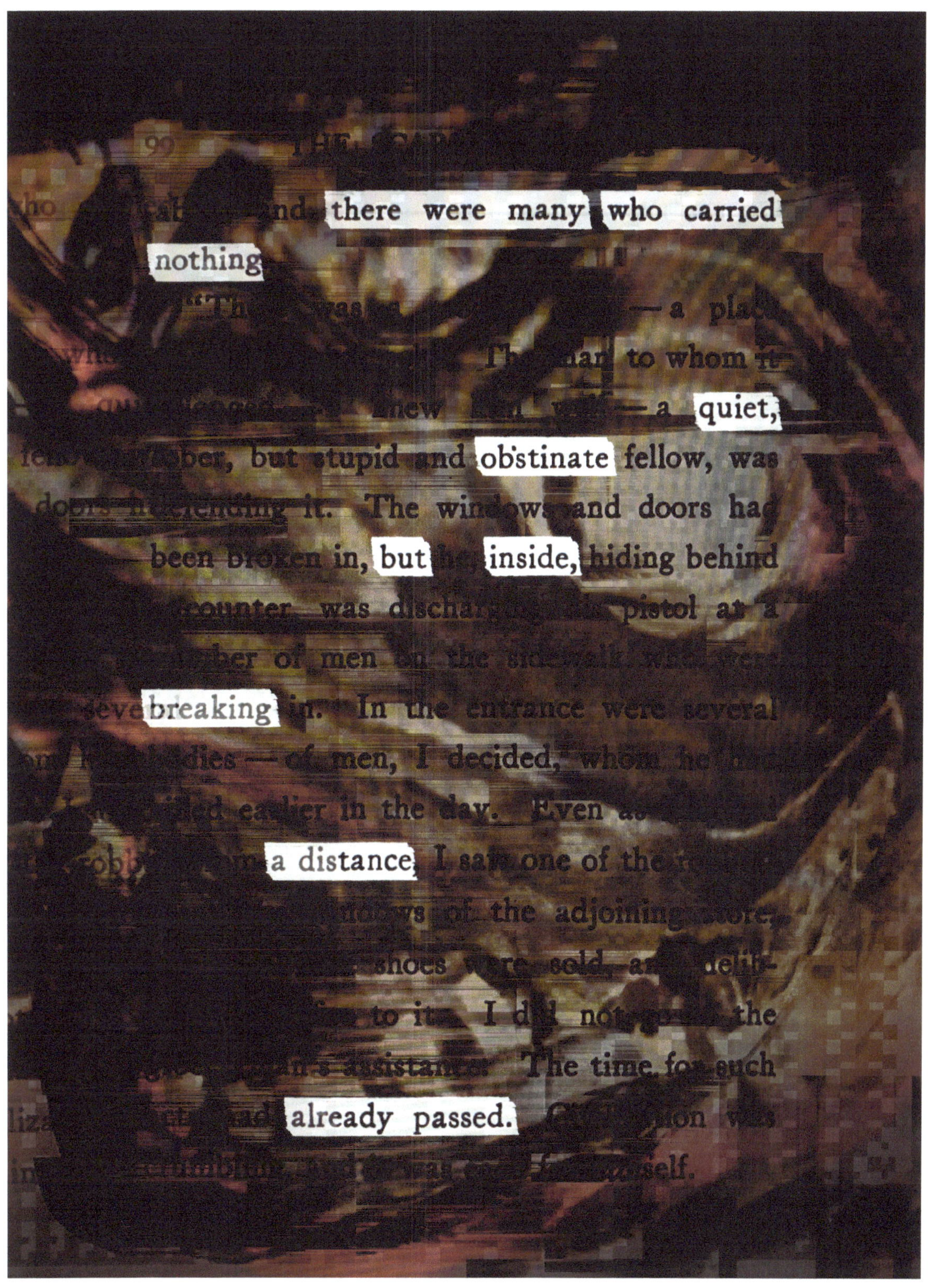
there were many who carried
nothing
a quiet,
obstinate fellow, was
but inside, hiding behind
breaking
a distance
already passed.

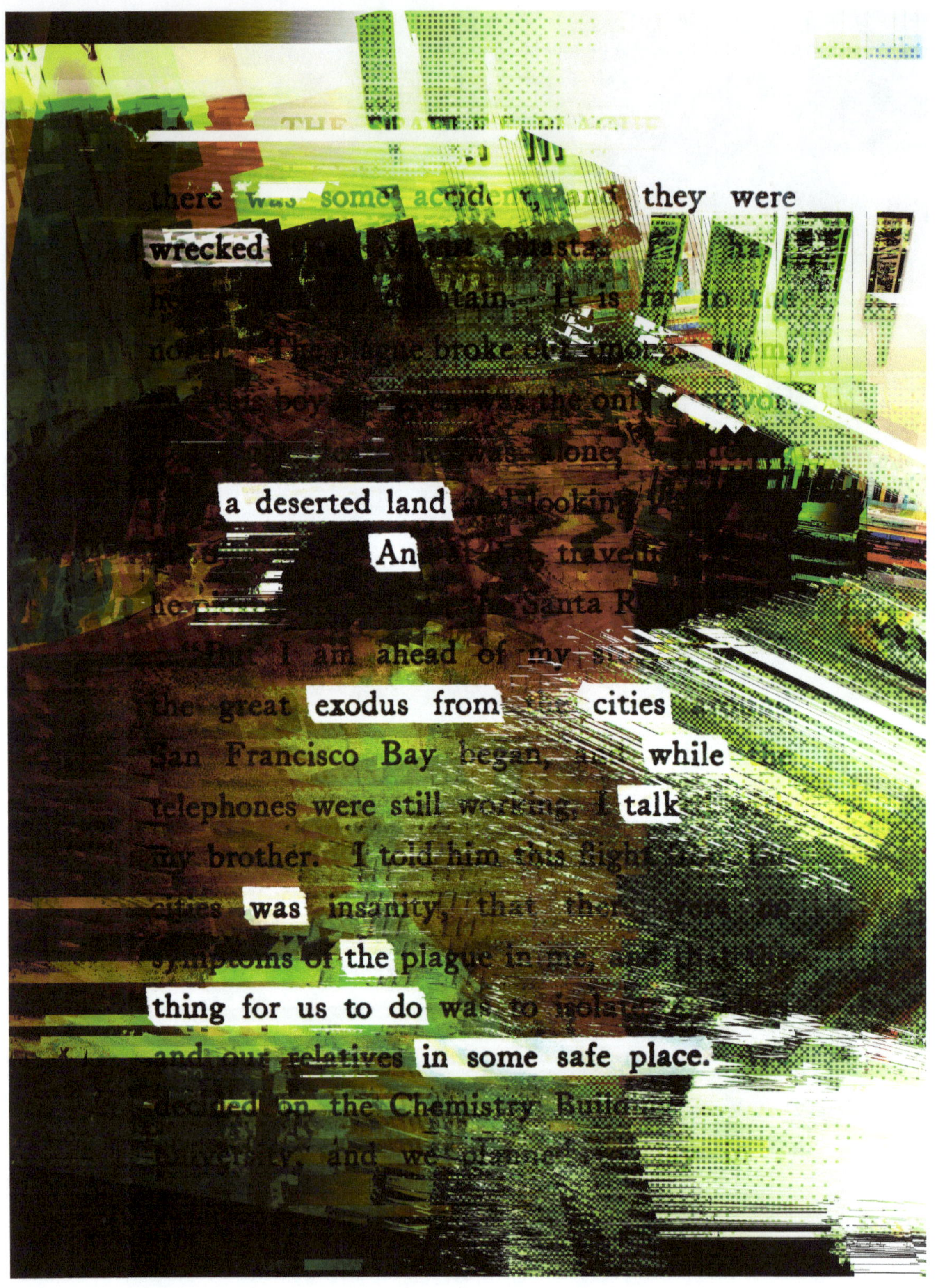
wrecked
a deserted land
An
exodus from the cities
while
talk
was
thing for us to do
in some safe place.

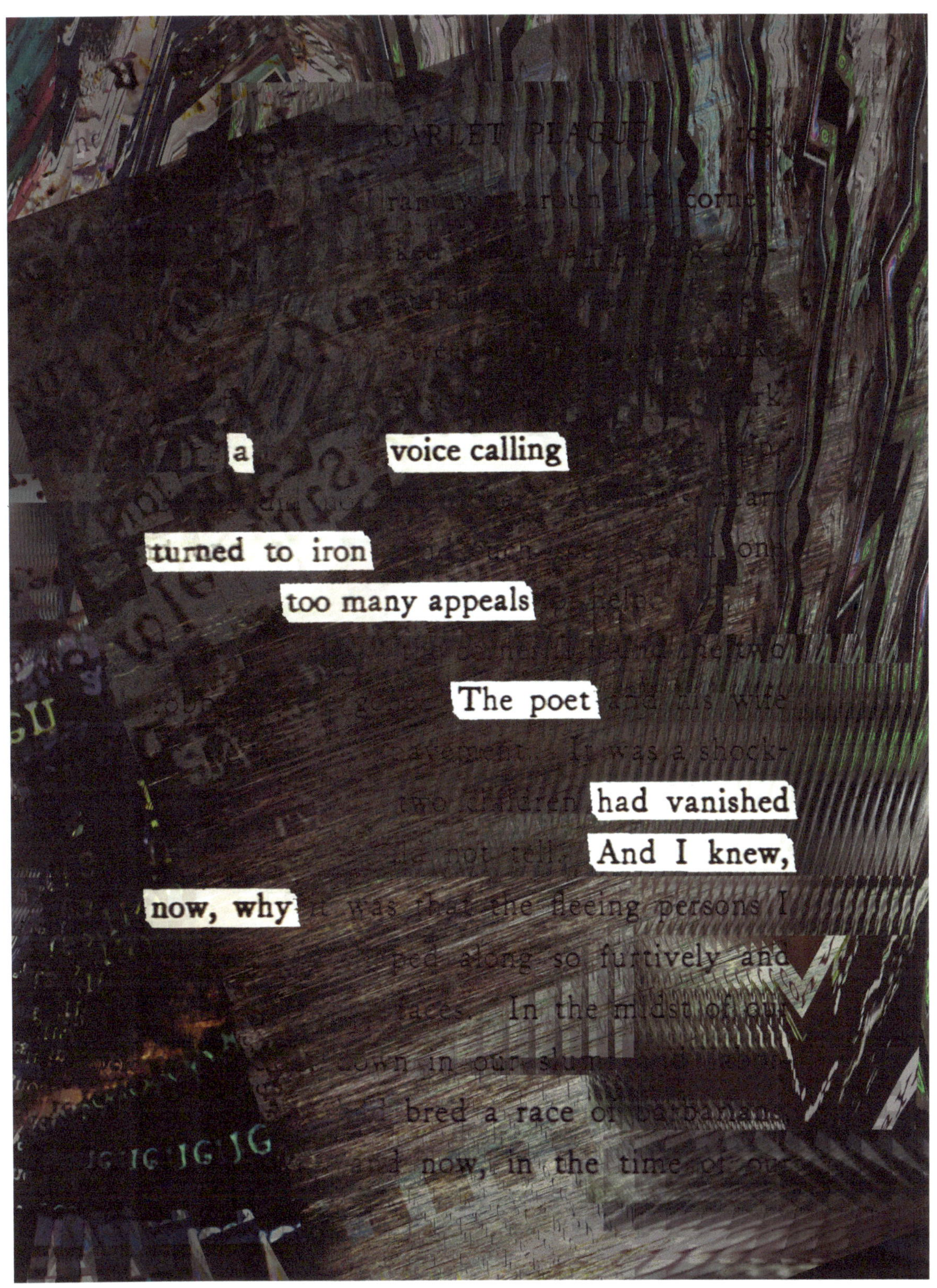
a   voice calling
turned to iron
too many appeals
The poet
had vanished
And I knew,
now, why

98   THE SCARLET PLAGUE

at the midburning filled the heavens, so that the mid-
day was as a gloomy twilight, and in the
shifts of wind, sometimes the sun shone
through dimly, a dull red orb. Truly, my
grandsons, it was like the last days of the
end of the world.

Everywhere there were numerous stalled motor cars,
showing that the gasoline and the engine
out. The supplies of the garages had given out. I re-
and a woman member one such car. A man and a woman
on the palay back dead in the seats, and on the pave-
women and ment near it were two more women and a
child. Strange and terrible sights there were
here and there on every hand. People slipped by silently,
furtively, like ghosts — white-faced women
carrying infants in their arms; fathers
leading children by the hand, singly,
and in couples, and in families — all flee-
ing out of the city of death. Some carried
supplies of food, others blankets and valu-

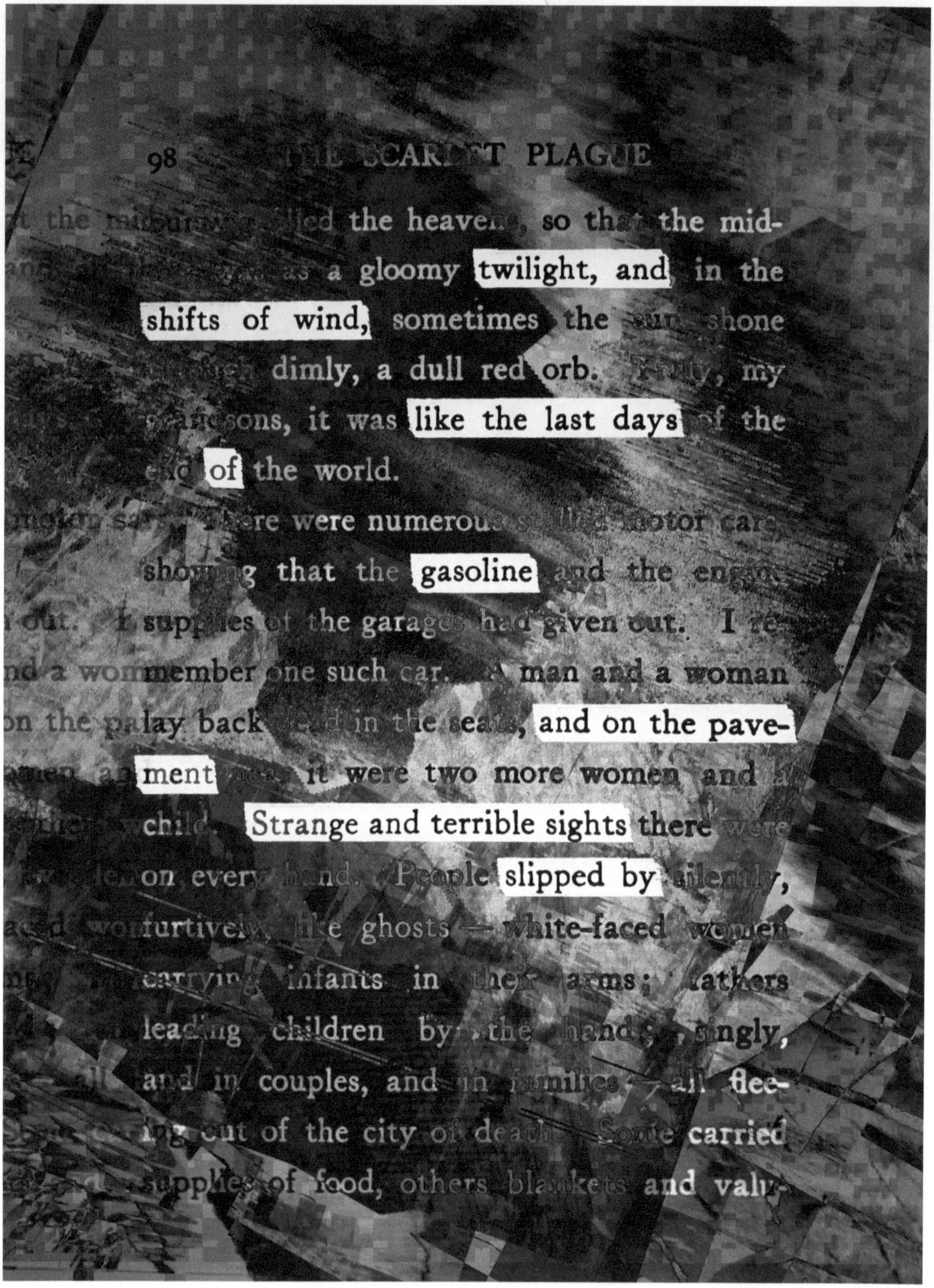

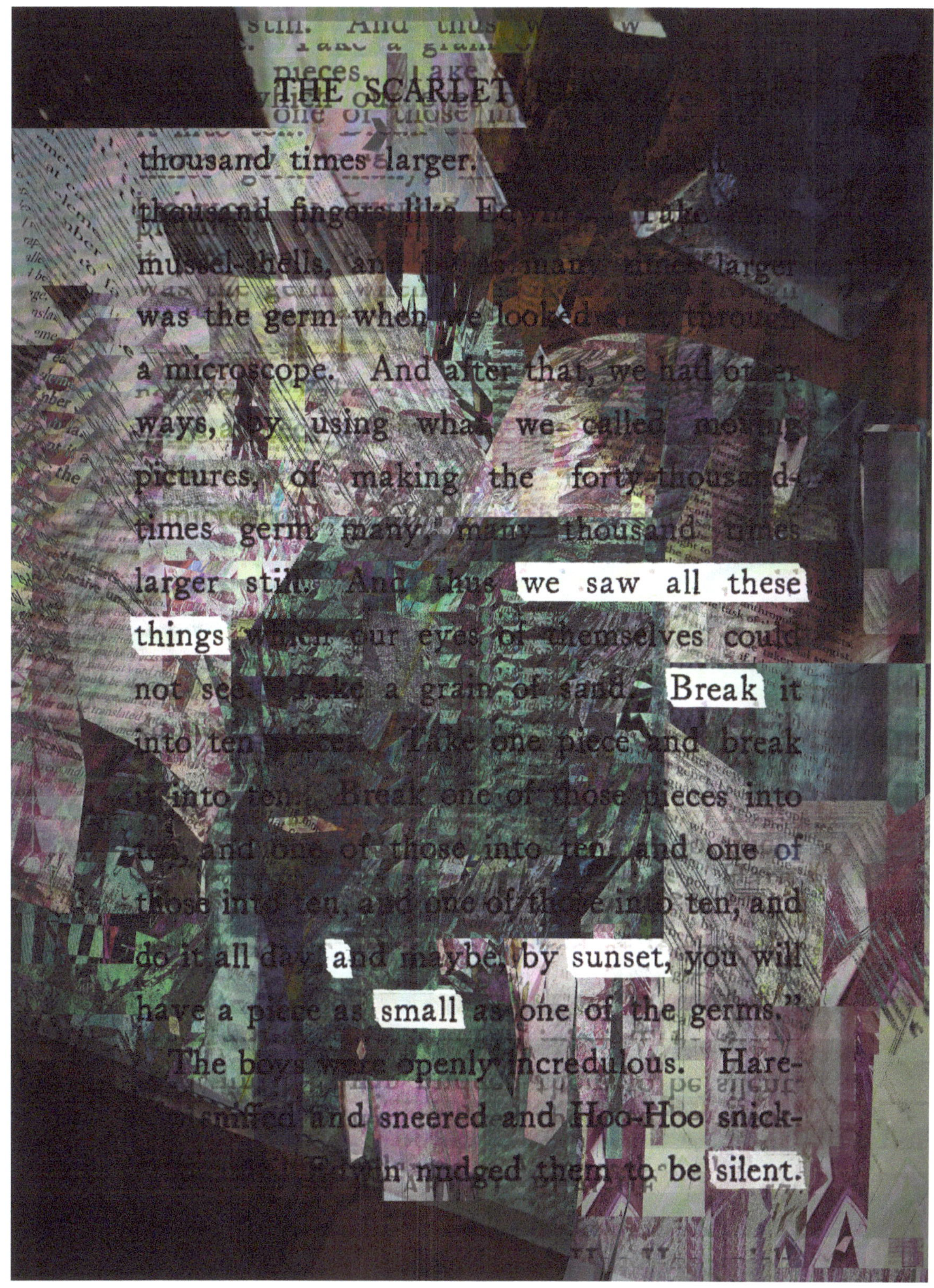
THE SCARLET

thousand times larger.
thousand fingers like Egypt. Take
mussel-shells, and just as many times larger
was the germ when we looked at it through
a microscope. And after that, we had other
ways, by using what we called moving
pictures, of making the forty-thousand-
times germ many, many thousand times
larger still. And thus we saw all these
things which our eyes of themselves could
not see. Take a grain of sand. Break it
into ten pieces. Take one piece and break
it into ten. Break one of those pieces into
ten, and one of those into ten, and one of
those into ten, and one of those into ten, and
do it all day and maybe by sunset, you will
have a piece as small as one of the germs."
The boys were openly incredulous. Hare-
lip sniffed and sneered and Hoo-Hoo snick-
ered until Edwin nudged them to be silent.

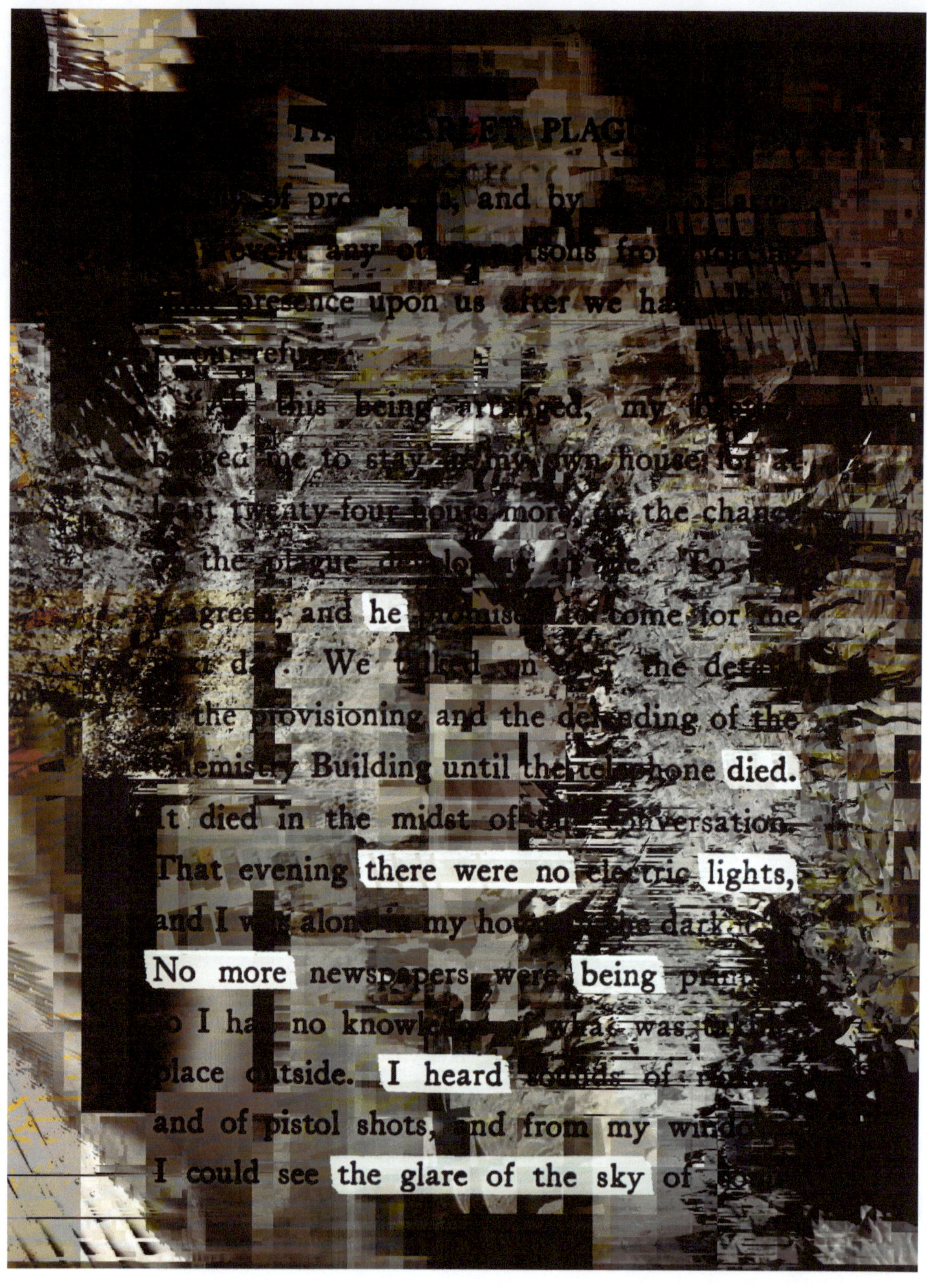
THE SCARLET PLAGUE
of provisions, and by
prevent any other persons from forcing
presence upon us after we ha
our refuge.
this being arranged, my
me to stay in my own house for at
least twenty-four hours more, on the chance
of the plague developing in me. To
agreed, and he promised to come for me
day. We talked on the deta
the provisioning and the defending of the
Chemistry Building until the telephone died.
It died in the midst of our conversation.
That evening there were no electric lights,
and I was alone in my house in the dark.
No more newspapers were being print
So I had no knowledge of what was taking
place outside. I heard sounds of riot
and of pistol shots, and from my window
I could see the glare of the sky of

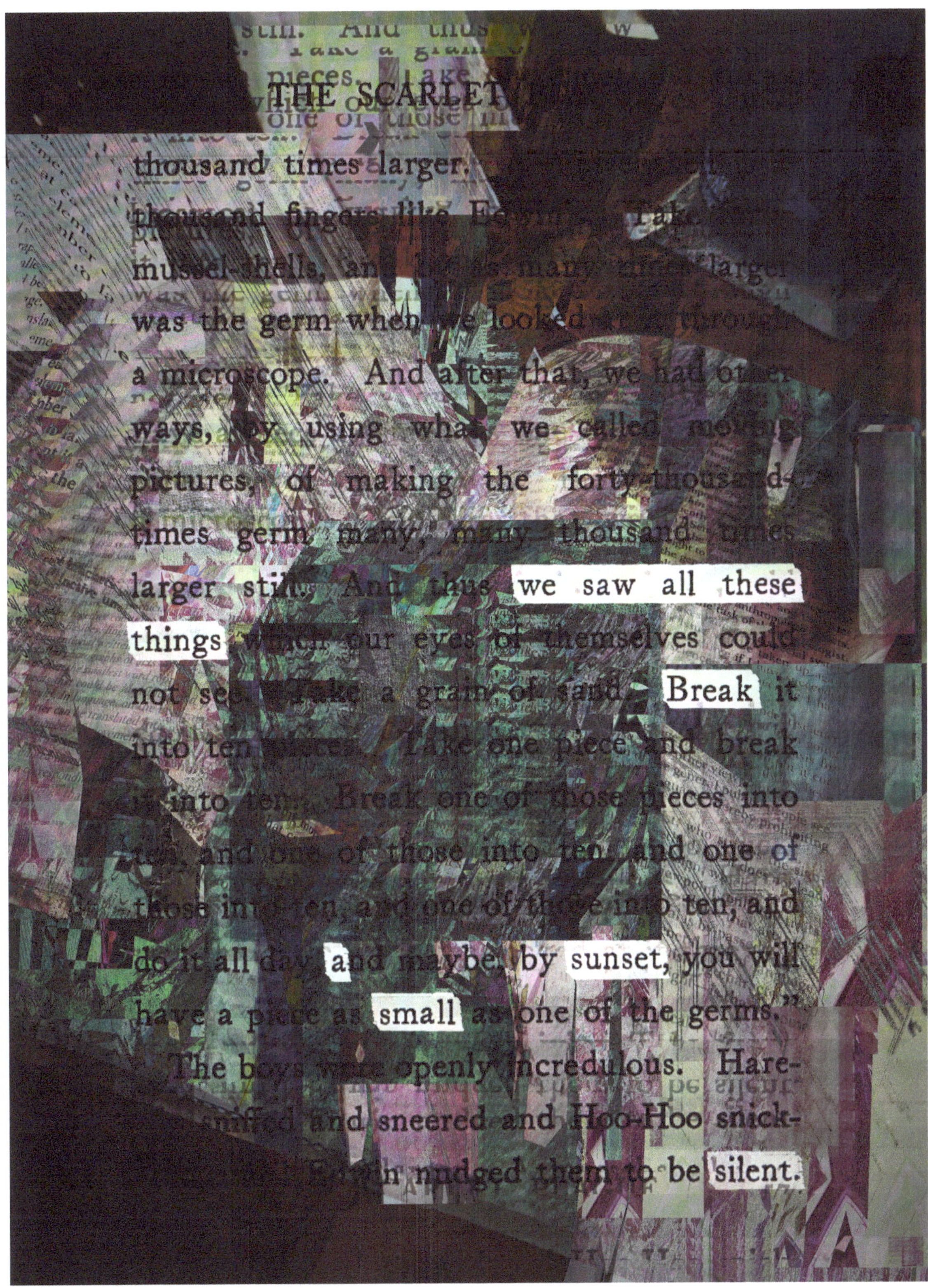

THE SCARLET

thousand times larger. thousand fingers like Eskimos. Take mussel-shells, and but as many times larger was the germ when we looked at it through a microscope. And after that, we had other ways, by using what we called moving pictures, of making the forty-thousand-times germ many, many thousand times larger still. And thus we saw all these things which our eyes of themselves could not see. Take a grain of sand. Break it into ten pieces. Take one piece and break it into ten. Break one of those pieces into ten, and one of those into ten, and one of those into ten, and one of those into ten, and do it all day and maybe, by sunset, you will have a piece as small as one of the germs."

The boys were openly incredulous. Hare-sniffed and sneered and Hoo-Hoo snick- Edwin nudged them to be silent.

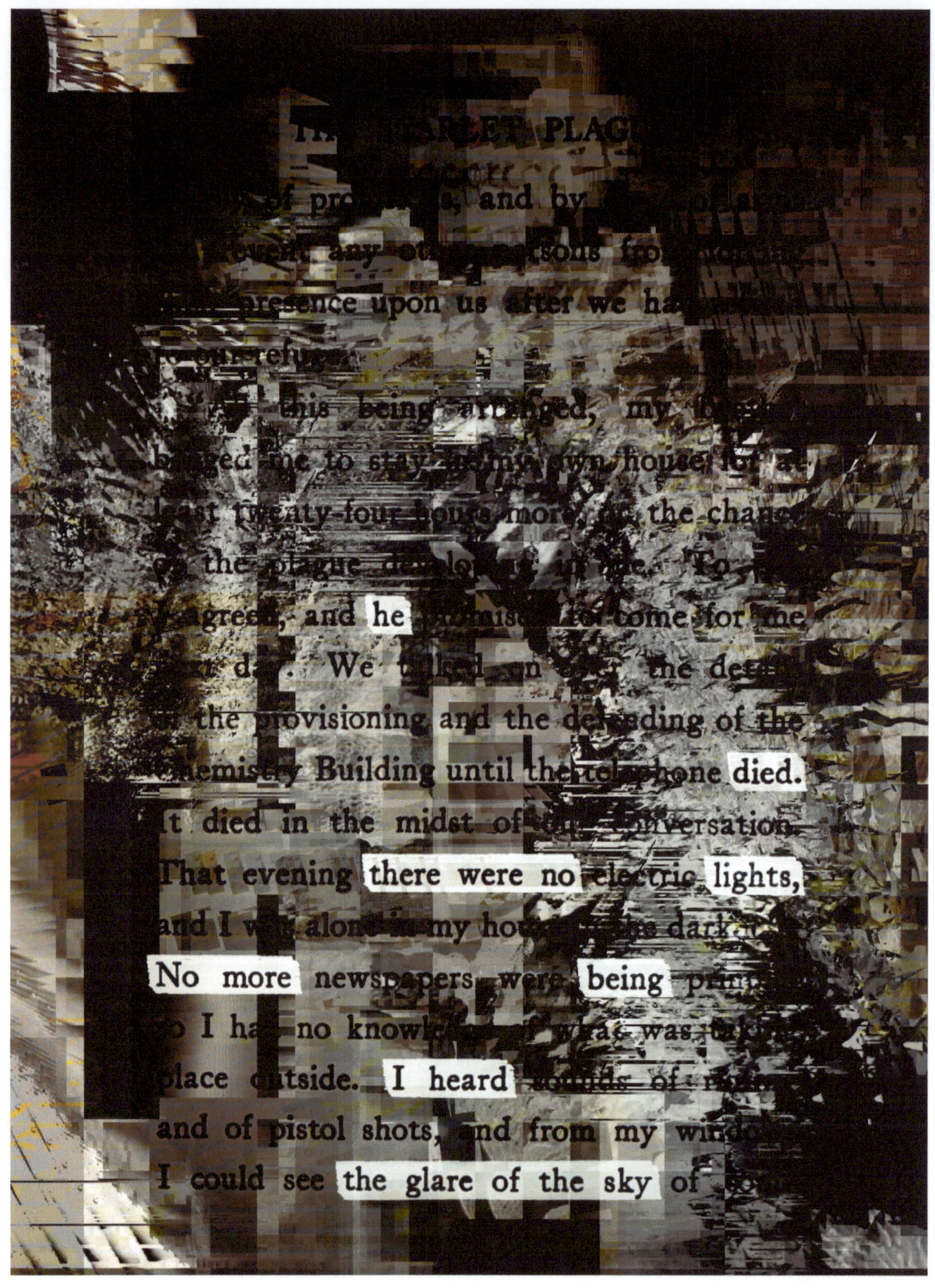
prevent any other persons from forcing
presence upon us after we ha
our refuge.
this being arranged, my
ged me to stay in my own house for at
least twenty-four hours more, on the chance
of the plague developing in me. To
agreed, and he promised to come for me
day. We talked over the det
the provisioning and the defending of the
Chemistry Building until the telephone died.
It died in the midst of our conversation.
That evening there were no electric lights,
and I was alone in my house in the dark.
No more newspapers were being prin
so I had no knowledge of what was taking
place outside. I heard sounds of riot
and of pistol shots, and from my window
I could see the glare of the sky of

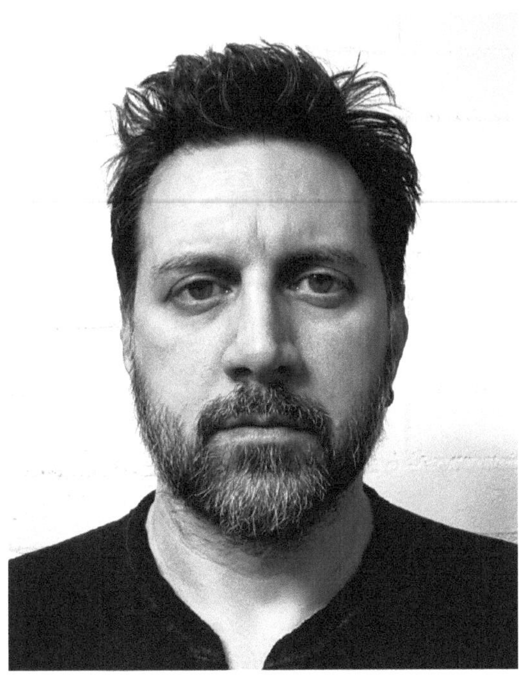

Francesco Levato is a poet, literary translator, new media artist, and writer of speculative fiction. Recent books include *SCARLET*; *Arsenal/Sin Documentos*; *Endless, Beautiful, Exact*; *Elegy for Dead Languages*; *War Rug*; *Creaturing* (as translator); and the chapbooks *A Continuum of Force* and *jettison/collapse*. Recent speculative fiction appears in various publications, including *Savage Planets, Sci-Fi Shorts,* and *Tales to Terrify.* He has collaborated and performed with various composers, including Philip Glass, and his cinépoetry has been exhibited in galleries and featured at film festivals in Berlin, Chicago, New York, and elsewhere. He holds an MFA in Poetry, a PhD in English Studies, and is currently an Associate Professor of Literature & Writing Studies at California State University San Marcos.

www.ingramcontent.com/pod-product-compliance
Lightning Source LLC
Chambersburg PA
CBHW042113030726
47599CB00002B/199